Roll Around a Point

by

duane cole

W9-DCS-144

REVISED EDITION

COPYRIGHT 1976

BY DUANE COLE

PRINTED IN THE UNITED STATES OF AMERICA

ALL RIGHTS RESERVED

PUBLISHED BY KEN COOK COMPANY

MILWAUKEE, WISCONSIN

CONTENTS

WHY AEROBATICS

Why aerobatics? It is a good question to which there are two simple answers. First, aerobatics are fun. Secondly, pilots trained in aerobatics are safer pilots by virtue of their knowledge of the adversities of the aircraft and smoother pilots because of improved coordination and feel of the controls.

Let's talk a little about the second answer. Pilots are being turned out by the thousands without the slightest idea of the consequences of full application of the wheel or rudder pedals. It is true that an airplane can be taken off and flown from point A to point B and landed with only a slight movement of the controls. It is also true that an automobile can be driven from city A to city B with only a slight movement of the steering wheel. Yet, we would not consider allowing a loved one to be a passenger in a car driven by a person not skilled in the extreme use of the steering wheel, accelerator, and brakes.

An airplane is designed to rotate around each of its three axes. Isn't it then reasonable to assume that a pilot trained to control an airplane throughout these rotations is a safer pilot? Of course it is. It may happen only once in a life time, or once in ten life times, but pilots will inadvertently get their aircraft into un-usual positions from which safe recovery is dependent upon their knowledge of aerobatics. It happened to me when I had 14,000 hours of flying time.

Arriving back in Fort Wayne after a dual cross country flight in a 250 Comanche, my student called the tower and was told we would be number two to land on run-way 22 following a United DC-7. It was one of those calm summer evenings with-out a wisp of air to rile the smoke ascending vertically from the factories east of town. Noting this condition, I cautioned my student about the dangers of vortignous air created by large aircraft such as the one preceding us. I further explained that with no air movement to break it up or carry it away, its dissipation rate would be very slow. Taking what I thought was ample precaution, the student planned his approach so that we were two miles out on final as the airliner made its touchdown. When the United Captain turned off the runway, we were down to 500 feet and still a mile out. I was sitting relaxed, watching the Captain with jealous admiration. He had been farsighted enough to join the airlines at a time when I thought I could make my fortune in airport operations and other non-revenue-producing aviation activities. Then it happened. With no warning, we found ourselves inverted with the nose down at a 30° angle. Instinctively, I grabbed the wheel and executed a half roll to the upright position, recovering just a hundred feet above Jim Kelley's golf course. I have never been one to ride the controls with a student in the left seat, so in retrospect I cannot say whether the young man abetted the rolling action of the turbulence by jerking the wheel over or not. But I do know this --- we did go upside down and had I not been capable of slow rolling, we would have been killed.

Let me cite another authenticated instance of this nature. This story had its beginning back in April of 1942 when I applied for a civilian flight instructor's job at War Eagle Field at Lancaster, California. I was given my check ride by a flight commander who was to become the hero of this incident. The most impressive thing about this man (I will call him Bill) was the ease and precision with which he demonstrated aerobatic maneuvers.

At the time, War Eagle Field was the home of Polaris Flight Academy where Royal Air Force pilots were being trained on the Lend-Lease agreement with Great Britain. Most of the instructors had gone there because they liked the versatility of the British curriculum and I was no exception. Here there was a certain amount of leeway allowed in training methods that was not permitted under the rigid flight training standards of USAAF contract flying schools. So in 1943, when the school was converted to an American basic training program, many of the instructors resigned. Some of them, like Bill, went with the airlines.

WHY
AEROBATICS   I lost track of Bill until years later when I read in the paper about the near crash of an airliner on which he was Captain. He was cruising along in the clear sky of western Texas with a plane load of contented passengers when the wheel jerked forward and the airplane nosed over. By the time Bill could recover the wheel and get the four throttles closed, the huge machine had gone past the vertical position, descending at an unprecedented rate of speed. Having no alternative, he applied forward pressure until the airplane reached the inverted position and then rolled out just above the sage brush. The cause of this wild ride, a goof on the part of one of the crew in adjusting the elevator trim, is not important to this story, but the fact that only a pilot with an aerobatic background could have recovered from it, is.

Since you did not buy this book to read hairy yarns -- at least, we hope you didn't -- but to learn something about aerobatics, I will forego the urge to continue story telling and get on with imparting what knowledge I have of the aerobatic science.

Undoubtedly, you have heard pilots telling of doing aerobatics in standard category airplanes. Chances are they are telling the truth, but this does not make such actions advisable. Accomplished aerobatic pilots execute maneuvers with a minimum of G forces so may be able to demonstrate the controlability of an airplane not certificated for aerobatics without damaging it. I have witnessed aerobatic demonstrations by Bevo Howard and my brother Marion in Model 35 Bonanzas, yet with this airplane's record of wing failures, it would be fool-hardy for the average pilot to attempt such a demonstration.

WHY A REVISED EDITION?

In 1965 when I first published ROLL AROUND A POINT, the only available aerobatic trainers were of World War II or earlier vintage. Meyers, Ryans, Great Lakes, Fairchilds, Wacos, and Stearmans were the planes most commonly used. They did the job they were designed to do but didn't compare well with the modern aerobatic trainer. Oh, they were strong enough. As a matter of fact, they probably would have sustained more G loads than some of our new trainers but their advantage ends there. Their controls were heavier and not nearly so responsive and most were underpowered with engines not equipped to run while the airplane was inverted. Of course, I didn't mind the engine not running while the airplane was upside down. Since 1940, I have done an air show routine with the engine shut off. As I used to tell my students -- the wings don't know the propeller isn't turning. The only thing they are interested in is the airflow over their surfaces. However, to maintain altitude and get the most out of a practice period an inverted system is sure nice.

Like the old airplanes, as evidenced by the diagrams, there was really nothing wrong with the first edition of ROLL AROUND A POINT, but it was written with a Stearman in mind and now, eleven years later, we do our training in Decathlons, Pitts, the new Great Lakes, and others certified aerobatic by the FAA. So to keep pace with the industry I have done this revision.

INTRODUCTION TO AEROBATICS

Some readers may have learned to fly back in the days when learning to fly was more important than learning the functions of a radio and consequently know something about the basic aerobatic maneuvers. However, I must assume that most are products of the New Look in aviation and will try to teach accordingly. This course is only ten hours long and will be all dual instruction. It is possible to learn aerobatics by yourself, but for various reasons it is definitely not advisable.

On the first flight and all subsequent flights, we will climb out to a minimum of three thousand feet and get somewhere off the airways. It is usually possible to find an area nearby where aerobatics can be done without violating civil air regulations, but there are some cities so surrounded with controlled areas it is difficult to find a legal place to practice. Even though you might not feel guilty about committing such a violation, to keep from getting stuck with a stiff fine and maybe the loss of your license it is better to abide by the rules. Many fellows, finding they are using all their gasoline going to and from the practice area, move their plane to an airport more ideally located and drive back and forth.

This first hour is designed to give you a new concept of control movements and to relieve any apprehension you may have about so called unusual positions. To get you better acquainted with the stick and rudder, we will start our lessons with a coordination exercise. This will entail rolling the airplane from side to side while keeping the nose pointed straight ahead. As the stick moves laterally the rudder corrections for adverse yaw will at times be applied in the direction of the stick and at times in the opposite direction. Coordination of the stick and rudder

7

does not always mean that they will be moved in the same direction. It means they will be used in whatever manner is necessary to produce the desired reaction of the airplane.

Since the maneuver is practiced on a straight course, we must, as in all our maneuvering, be careful not to exceed the limits of the designated practice area. In addition to its value as a coordination exercise, it is a good loosening up maneuver, so we will do it every time we go up.

To get the feel of a strange airplane, I like to include in my checkout a series of steep turns -- steep tight turns that ride on the edge of a high speed stall. I believe they show more about the characteristics of an airplane than any other single maneuver. I also believe they tell more about a pilot's ability than any other single maneuver. We will do them in this course to get you better acquainted with the airplane and as a training maneuver.

Enter the maneuver as you would a medium bank and turn, increasing the bank as the turn progresses. As the degree of bank increases, so does the amount of back pressure needed to hold the airplane in the turn. In a like manner, increased back pressure proportionately increases the G forces on both the airplane and the pilot. When the airplane can be banked no steeper and still hold its altitude and the back pressure is so great that an increase would cause a stall, hold the turn until you have completed 720° of turning. If while in the turn your vision becomes blurred, roll out. This fuzziness is an indication of an impending blackout, so ease up on the G load by making your next turn slightly more shallow. Steep turns should never be practiced for extensive periods. They can become nauseating.

Everyone who flys knows the value of practicing different stall maneuvers. They are used in all training programs and given on every flight test. In this course, we are going to revive a couple of them that have been discarded in recent years. They are altitude losing maneuvers and, like others of that nature, must not be started until a survey of the area, paying special attention to the air space below, is made by two 90° clearing turns.

To execute the first one, close the throttle and bring the nose up to 60° above the horizon and hold it there. As the speed dissipates and the flow of air over the wings decreases, you will find the ailerons losing their effectiveness, necessitating the increased use of rudder to hold the wings level. When the stall occurs, release the back pressure on the stick and push forward. Hold the airplane in a dive until it gains flying speed, then bring it back to straight and level and open the throttle to cruise power.

At the break of the stall and as the nose is going down, you will experience the rather pleasant sensation of weightlessness. You will be convinced there is room for your stomach in your chest cavity because it was just there. I demonstrated this stall to my son Rolly when he was three years old. As we pushed over, he cried out "Whoopee". From that day on, my kids have begged me to do whoopee stalls.

After regaining the altitude lost while practicing a series of the power-off stalls, we will try some with cruising power. In doing the power-on version, you will find the airplane holding its climb longer and requiring the use of right rudder to control the rolling effect of engine and prop while approaching the stall and left rudder to control the lack of it after the break. Recovery is made by pushing over into the same 45° dive and holding it until cruising airspeed is reached before returning the airplane to normal flight.

Next comes the full oscillation stall -- the best of all rudder exercise maneuvers. Like the whoopee stalls, this is done both with and without power. With level wings, once again bring the nose up to 60° above the horizon. When the aircraft stalls, bring the stick back to its most rearward position and hold it there. As the nose drops, the airplane will tend to fall off first in one direction, then the other. This will be prevented by keeping the nose straight with the rudder only. In any stall maneuver, including a landing, a wing cannot go down if the nose is not allowed to turn. With the changing attitude of the airplane, after the stall starts, will come an increased flow of air over the wings increasing their lift and the effectiveness of the elevator. This, in turn, will cause the nose, which will have dropped below the horizon, to return to the level flight position. At this point, release the back pressure and return to normal flight. Full oscillation stalls literally keep you on your toes. Inadequate or belated use of the rudder may result in some pretty fantastic gyrations or even a spin. If this happens, release the back pressure, execute normal spin recovery, and start over.

I know that you have been a little apprehensive about spins, but you will be over your uneasiness as soon as you do one. A two-turn spin will use up about a thousand feet of altitude in most trainers, so make a very thorough check beneath us before starting. If it is all clear, close the throttle and bring the nose up to the normal power-off stall attitude and hold it there. As buffeting begins and you detect the approaching stall, apply full rudder in the direction you wish to spin and haul the stick back in your lap for full-up elevator. To keep yourself oriented, count by half-turns. At the end of two turns, with brisk positive action, kick in full opposite rudder to stop the rotation and pop the stick forward to break the stall. As soon as possible after the rotation stops, return the nose to normal flight attitude, thus eliminating any excessive build up of air speed. After you have completed a spin and found it more fun than frightening, you will be wondering why you had not learned them before. Although the stall-spin accident has been the greatest killer of all in general aviation, the spin itself is not dangerous. A spinning airplane is a free-falling object rotating about its vertical axis and is subject to no undue strain. The danger of a spin comes from the ignorance of it.

There are various reasons for an airplane capable of spinning refusing to spin. The most likely of these being poor timing of control usage during the entry. If full rudder is applied too early or if the stall occurs before rudder is used, a spiral will result. A spiral imposes loads on the pilot and airplane that can become dangerously high. Break a spiral immediately by releasing the back pressure and rolling out with rudder and aileron.

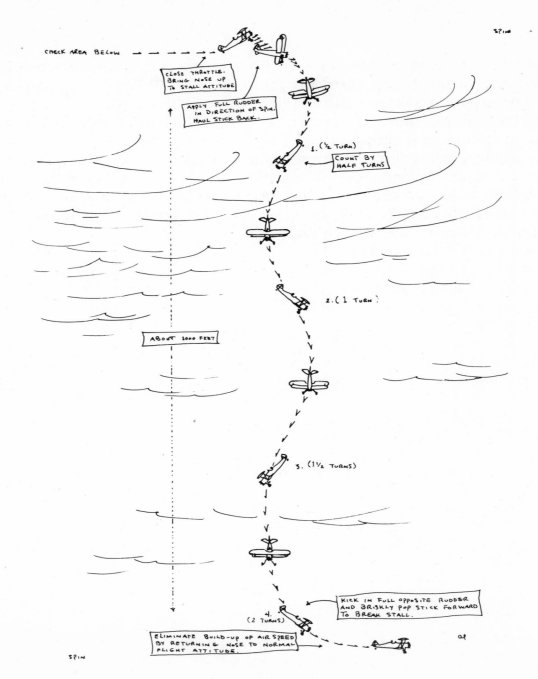

SPIN

CHECK AREA BELOW ------

CLOSE THROTTLE.
BRING NOSE UP
TO STALL ATTITUDE.

APPLY FULL RUDDER
IN DIRECTION OF SPIN.
HAUL STICK BACK.

1. (½ TURN)

COUNT BY
HALF TURNS

2. (1 TURN)

ABOUT 1000 FEET

3. (1½ TURNS)

KICK IN FULL OPPOSITE RUDDER
AND BRISKLY POP STICK FORWARD
TO BREAK STALL.

4.
(2 TURNS)

ELIMINATE BUILD-UP OF AIR SPEED
BY RETURNING NOSE TO NORMAL
FLIGHT ATTITUDE.

SPIN

11

Recovery attempted without an abrupt use of the controls may not stop the spin, but contrarily, popping the stick too far forward may result in a sloppy recovery with an unnecessary loss of altitude and an excessive build-up of speed. Rudder used to stop the rotation may start the spin in the opposite direction if continued after the rotation has stopped. As you can see, clean entries and positive recoveries are both a matter of timing. Spins should be practiced in both directions, so after doing one, climb back to altitude and do one the other way. Because of CG locations, it is recommended that some airplanes not be spun. As in all maneuvers described in this book, spins will be practiced only in airplanes approved for such maneuvers by the manufacturer.

ON TO THE LOOP AND IMMELMANN

Following a review of the maneuvers previously introduced, we will get started with Chandelles and Lazy Eights, both excellent training maneuvers. They will help develop your coordination and build up your sense of timing.

To get the feel of the plane while maneuvering from excessive speed to just above a stall we will begin the Chandelle with a dive. With cruise power and the nose down about 30° we will let the air speed build up to 20 mph above cruising speed then roll into a 30° bank and turn. While banking the airplane must be held in the dive with forward pressure. To let the nose come up would spoil the maneuver. When the bank is established we will come straight back on the stick and increase the throttle proportionate to the climb. Since this portion of the maneuver is part of a loop in an oblique plane, there should be no variance of the bank. Continue the pull-up until you have turned 90°. At this point, with coordinated stick and rudder, begin the roll out paying particular attention to maintaining the established angle of climb. At 180° from the point of entry, the wings should be level and the airplane in a climbing attitude at just above stalling speed. Lower the nose to level flight and reduce the throttle to complete the maneuver.

Most aerobatic maneuvers seem to be more easily performed to the left than to the right. The reasons for this are both physical and psychological, but whatever the reasons, the best way to overcome the tendency to conform is to repeat a maneuver executed in one direction with one in the other direction.

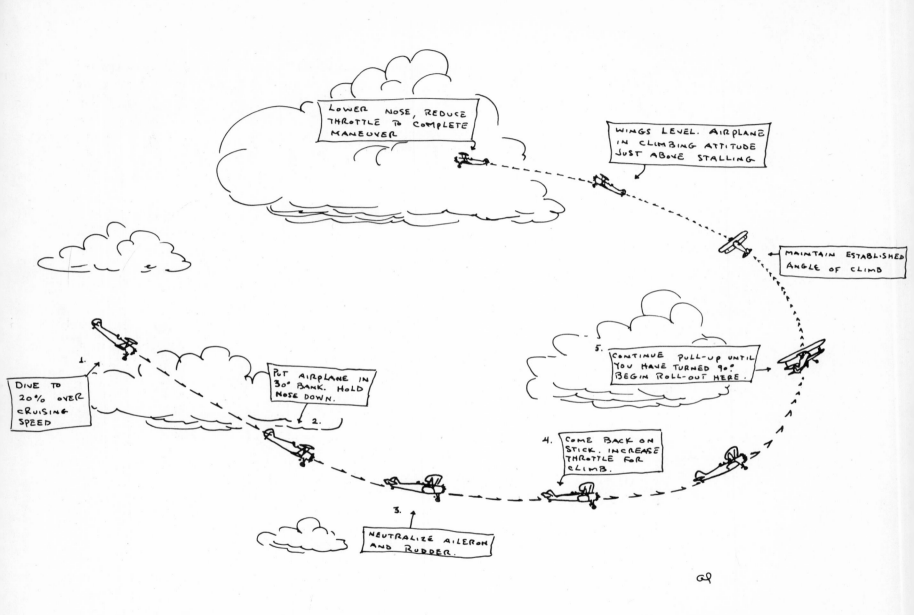

LOWER NOSE, REDUCE THROTTLE TO COMPLETE MANEUVER

WINGS LEVEL. AIRPLANE IN CLIMBING ATTITUDE JUST ABOVE STALLING

MAINTAIN ESTABLISHED ANGLE OF CLIMB

5. CONTINUE PULL-UP UNTIL YOU HAVE TURNED 90°. BEGIN ROLL-OUT HERE.

1.

DIVE TO 20% OVER CRUISING SPEED

PUT AIRPLANE IN 30° BANK. HOLD NOSE DOWN.

2.

4. COME BACK ON STICK. INCREASE THROTTLE FOR CLIMB.

3.

NEUTRALIZE AILERON AND RUDDER.

CHANDELLE

14

Positioning, very important in airshow or competitive work, is equally important in practicing. A series of maneuvers without regard to positioning can soon take you past the boundaries of the assigned practice area. After an hour of practice, you could quite conceivably end up many miles from home. In order to hold your position while doing Chandelles, start the first maneuver with a left bank and turn into the wind. Completing a series of 4 or 5 of them to the left, we will do a like number to the right with our first turn into the wind.

The lazy eight is a training maneuver par excellence. In its execution as we will do it, climbs, dives, and turns are used throughout a speed range from 20% over cruising airspeed to 20% under cruising airspeed. Once the maneuver is started, it is in a continual state of change with control pressures varying constantly as the airplane climbs and dives through two continuing 180° turns started from opposite directions. For proper positioning, line the airplane up 90° to the wind. Looking along the wing or parallel to it, depending upon where you are sitting in the plane, pick a reference point on the horizon. Keeping this point in mind, with cruise power, lower the nose until attaining a speed 20% above cruising speed. (For the sake of clarification, we will use a cruising speed of 100 miles per hour which means our dive speed will be 120 miles per hour.) Now bring the nose up. As it passes through the horizon, begin a coordinated turn. Increase the rate of turn and back pressure simultaneously until the nose has turned 45°. From this attitude the nose is brought diagonally down through the spot we previously selected on the horizon. This is accomplished by reducing the amount of back pressure and slowly lessening the degree of bank. Immediately after the nose crosses the horizon the airplane must be eased into a bank in the other direction with an increase in back pressure to bring the nose back up. It should cross the horizon this time 180° from point of entry. At this juncture the wings should be momentarily level but already beginning to roll into the second half of the maneuver -- a replica of the first.

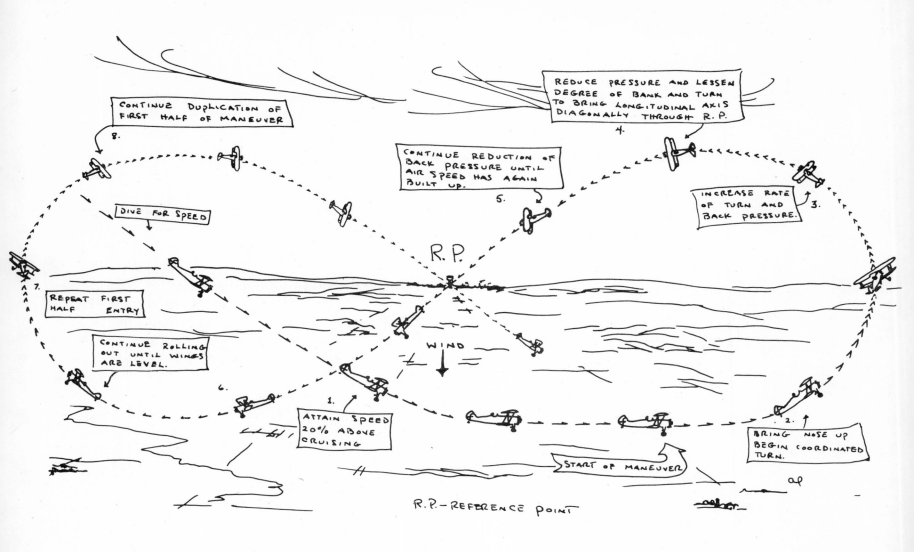

CONTINUE DUPLICATION OF
FIRST HALF OF MANEUVER
8.

REDUCE PRESSURE AND LESSEN
DEGREE OF BANK AND TURN
TO BRING LONGITUDINAL AXIS
DIAGONALLY THROUGH R.P.
4.

CONTINUE REDUCTION OF
BACK PRESSURE UNTIL
AIR SPEED HAS AGAIN
BUILT UP.
5.

DIVE FOR SPEED

INCREASE RATE
OF TURN AND
BACK PRESSURE.
3.

R.P.

REPEAT FIRST
HALF ENTRY
7.

CONTINUE ROLLING
OUT UNTIL WINGS
ARE LEVEL.
6.

WIND

1.
ATTAIN SPEED
20% ABOVE
CRUISING

2.
BRING NOSE UP
BEGIN COORDINATED
TURN.

START OF MANEUVER

R.P.—REFERENCE POINT

LAZY EIGHT

16

The lazy eight perfectly executed will appear from the cockpit to describe a figure eight lying on its side with the horizon bisecting its two symmetrical loops. It is a rhythmic maneuver that cannot be accomplished by mechanical manipulations. Once the rhythm is established, perfection is possible.

The symmetry of both the Chandelle and the lazy eight is pretty much dependent on a smooth application of back pressure. In a loop, the use of proper elevator control is also the major factor in maintaining symmetry, but without coordinated use of the throttle, the finished product is more apt to resemble a half moon or at best an egg. Once again, I will remind you of the difference between an air show airplane and an underpowered trainer. I have always felt that a good aerobatic airplane must have a wide range between top speed and stalling speed. In many instances, this range can be widened by converting to a more powerful engine. To cite an example, a 220 horsepower Stearman has a top speed of 115 miles per hour and stalls around 50 or 55 miles per hour. In contrast, a Stearman powered with a Pratt and Whitney 450 horsepower Wasp Jr. has a top speed of 150 miles per hour with a stalling speed nearly identical to that of a 220 horsepower Stearman.

In all his looping maneuvers, whether inside or outside, my son Rolly could, with white smoke from his 450 horsepower Stearman, leave the most symmetrical figures in the sky that I have ever seen. From straight and level and at 120 miles per hour, he would execute a perfectly circular loop ending up in straight and level flight with 120 miles per hour. He was able to do this because of a wide range of speed and an excellent weight-to-horsepower ratio.

One of our old government manuals states that stalling out on the top of a loop is caused by pulling up too rapidly at the beginning of the maneuver. I disagree wholeheartedly. Most stalls in the top of a loop are caused by pulling up too slowly, thus establishing a perimeter so large the airplane cannot follow it.

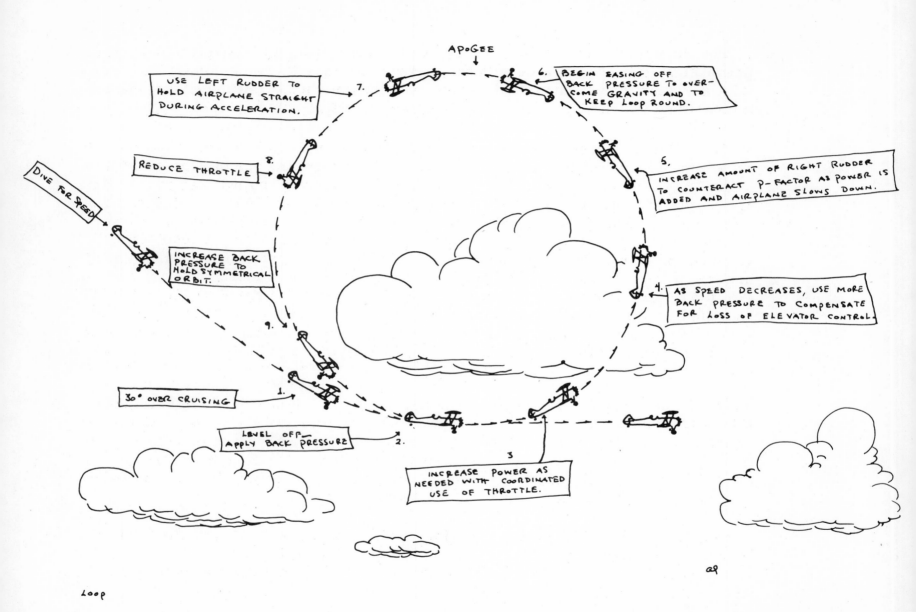

APOGEE

USE LEFT RUDDER TO HOLD AIRPLANE STRAIGHT DURING ACCELERATION.

7.

6. BEGIN EASING OFF BACK PRESSURE TO OVERCOME GRAVITY AND TO KEEP LOOP ROUND.

5. INCREASE AMOUNT OF RIGHT RUDDER TO COUNTERACT P-FACTOR AS POWER IS ADDED AND AIRPLANE SLOWS DOWN.

REDUCE THROTTLE   8.

DIVE FOR SPEED

INCREASE BACK PRESSURE TO HOLD SYMMETRICAL ORBIT.

4. AS SPEED DECREASES, USE MORE BACK PRESSURE TO COMPENSATE FOR LOSS OF ELEVATOR CONTROL.

9.

1.

30° OVER CRUISING

LEVEL OFF— APPLY BACK PRESSURE   2.

3

INCREASE POWER AS NEEDED WITH COORDINATED USE OF THROTTLE.

LOOP

18

To begin a loop, we will dive to gain additional momentum, but will not consider the dive as part of the maneuver. When 20% over cruising speed is reached, level off momentarily before applying back pressure. Increase the power as needed with a coordinated use of the throttle. Even with added power, the speed will decrease on the way up making it necessary to use more back pressure to compensate for loss of elevator control. You will note that an increased amount of rudder will also be required to keep the airplane straight. Approaching the top of the loop, the airplane will slow down and gravitational pull become greater as the centrifugal force is lessened. To overcome these effects and to keep the loop round let up on the back pressure about 15° before reaching the top. At 15° after passing the apogee of the loop back pressure must be reapplied to keep it nice and symmetrical on the back side. As right rudder was used to keep the airplane straight while it was climbing left rudder will be used to keep it straight while it is coming down. As the airplane picks up speed coming down the back side we will reduce throttle. Cutting back on the power will, in turn, reduce the G-Force resulting from the increased back pressure.

I prefer a progressive method of teaching and a natural progression leads us to the Immelman turn. It is my understanding that this maneuver was first executed by a German, Count Immelman, as an evasive action to elude the likes of Captain Eddie Rickenbacker and others who got on his tail during the air war over France in World War I.

The Immelman can be described as a half loop with a half roll recovery 180° from its direction of entry. The dive for speed and the pull up are done in much the same manner as those in a loop. However, to provide for more speed at the top, a greater speed must be attained in the dive. In an Immelman, you will be hanging on your belt for the first time. It will be an entirely new experience. The first time I hung upside down out of an airplane I was pretty scared. It happened on my first airplane ride. I was just sitting there enjoying the scenery when this old-timer I was riding with decided to roll the airplane. As we went

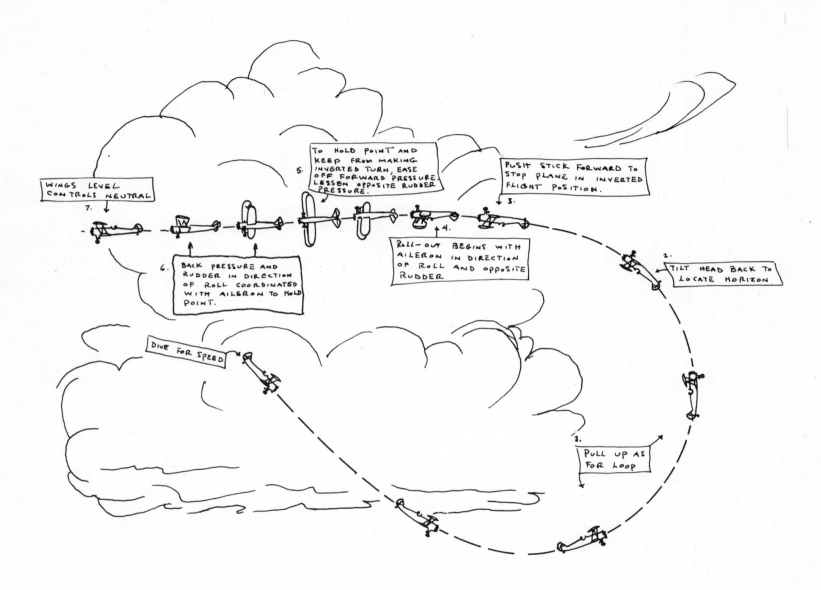

To HOLD POINT AND KEEP FROM MAKING INVERTED TURN, EASE OFF FORWARD PRESSURE LESSEN OPPOSITE RUDDER PRESSURE.

PUSH STICK FORWARD TO STOP PLANE IN INVERTED FLIGHT POSITION.

WINGS LEVEL CONTROLS NEUTRAL

BACK PRESSURE AND RUDDER IN DIRECTION OF ROLL COORDINATED WITH AILERON TO HOLD POINT.

Roll—OUT BEGINS WITH AILERON IN DIRECTION OF ROLL AND OPPOSITE RUDDER

TILT HEAD BACK TO LOCATE HORIZON

DIVE FOR SPEED

PULL UP AS FOR LOOP

IMMELMAN

20

over, my feet came off the floor, my hands flew out of the cockpit and due to a loose belt, I almost followed them. Boy! I thought I was a goner. From that day on, I have never intentionally tried to frighten any one who was my passenger or student.

Of course, you will not undergo the same sensations as I did. You will have one hand on the stick and the other on the throttle and your feet will be applying pressure to the rudder pedals. Above all, your belt will be tight. When I am doing a show, I like to tighten my belt as tight as possible and then tighten it some more. The tighter your belt is, the more you become a part of the airplane.

To get back to our lesson -- following the dive and the pull up and as you are approaching the top of the loop, tilt your head back to locate the horizon as soon as possible. As the nose reaches a position about 15° above the horizon push the stick forward to stop it there in the inverted flight attitude. In upside down flying gravity trying to pull the pilot out of the cockpit and the opposite reaction of his body make it seem difficult to move the stick forward. But this phenomenon can be overcome by using a tight belt and holding the upper part of the body slightly forward at the initial pull up.

From the inverted position we will get right side up by picking a point on the horizon and executing a half slow roll around it. Since rudder action is reversed when the airplane is inverted we will begin with aileron and opposite rudder. Forward pressure used to hold the nose up while inverted will be maintained until the wings have rolled to an attitude perpendicular to the horizon. As this knife edge position is approached opposite rudder pressure is reduced. At knife edge we will apply rudder in the direction of the aileron and gradually reduce forward pressure to allow the airplane to return to level flight horizontally as well as laterally.

HAMMERHEAD

The stall turn, more commonly called the hammerhead stall, is a beautiful maneuver to watch, especially when done in an airplane describing it with smoke. It is not a physically difficult maneuver to do, yet to accomplish it with precision requires a high degree of proficiency in planning and timing.

We will do our first hammerhead to the left. We will begin with a dive to about 10% above cruising speed then come back on the stick and add power. When the nose comes up through the horizon we will make sure our wings are level as it will be the last good reference over the nose until we reverse the direction of flight.

From this point on until the airplane is climbing vertically we will have to use a little right rudder to keep it straight. Also after passing through the horizon we will shift our field of vision from over the nose to our left wing (or wings). When the wing appears to be perpendicular to the horizon we will transition from back pressure to forward pressure to stop the airplane on a vertical line and to hold it there after the line is established. Just prior to the approaching stall we will apply full left rudder to pivot the airplane and enough right aileron to prevent the outside wing from developing lift and rolling in the direction of applied rudder.

The timing of the rudder is very critical. If its application comes too early the airplane will fly over the top as it would in a wing over. If it is applied too late the airplane will begin sliding backward before the rotation. If it is applied much too late the airplane will be in a full tail slide with its resultant whip stall. Tail slides and whip stalls are no-nos in most trainers. However, competition airplanes such as the Pitts seem to suffer no ill effects from them.

As the airplane changes its flight path from up to down, neutralize the rudder and aileron and close the throttle. To prevent an excessive build up of speed on the descent begin the pullout as soon as the vertical down line is established. In leveling off open the throttle to cruising rpm as you decelerate to cruising speed.

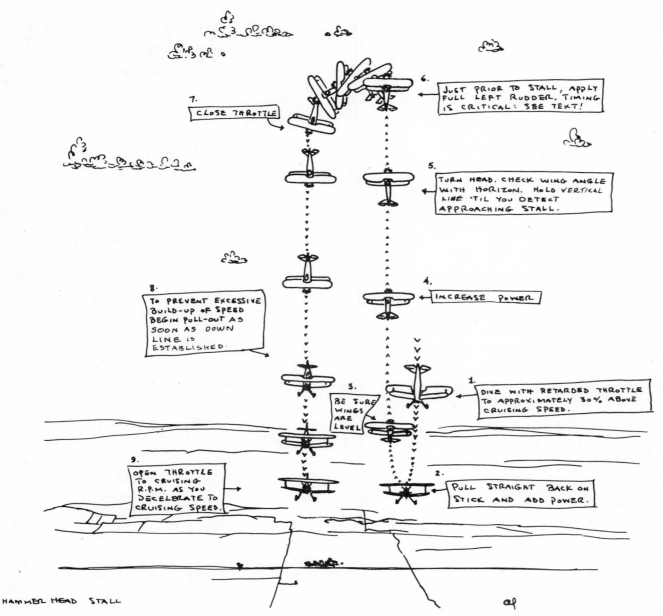

7.
CLOSE THROTTLE

6.
JUST PRIOR TO STALL, APPLY FULL LEFT RUDDER, TIMING IS CRITICAL! SEE TEXT!

5.
TURN HEAD. CHECK WING ANGLE WITH HORIZON. HOLD VERTICAL LINE 'TIL YOU DETECT APPROACHING STALL.

8.
TO PREVENT EXCESSIVE BUILD-UP OF SPEED BEGIN PULL-OUT AS SOON AS DOWN LINE IS ESTABLISHED.

4.
INCREASE POWER

3.
BE SURE WINGS ARE LEVEL

1.
DIVE WITH RETARDED THROTTLE TO APPROXIMATELY 30% ABOVE CRUISING SPEED.

9.
OPEN THROTTLE TO CRUISING R.P.M. AS YOU DECELERATE TO CRUISING SPEED.

2.
PULL STRAIGHT BACK ON STICK AND ADD POWER.

HAMMER HEAD STALL

A hammerhead to the right differs from that to the left as a result of engine and propeller forces. You will recall that in the first maneuver right rudder was necessary to hold the line straight. Also you will remember that we took advantage of the pull to the left by allowing the engine to continue its maximum output as we were rotating. But now that we plan to rotate to the right we will reduce the power to lessen that effect prior to applying rudder. This action requires split second timing. Closing the throttle will slow the climbing momentum immediately so the rudder must be used while there is still enough air passing over it to give it control.

CUBAN EIGHT

From the ground the Cuban Eight properly executed is seen as a figure eight lying on its side. As a matter of fact it is sometimes called a horizontal eight. Its execution might best be described as two continuing Immelmann turns with nose down recoveries entered from opposite headings. However, there are some differences between the Immelmann and one half a Cuban Eight. To begin with, the eight can be entered with ten percent less speed and secondly, it is stopped on a descending line as opposed to a horizontal line.

We will begin our dive and pull up as we would in an Immelmann but instead of stopping after completing half a loop we will continue on to a three quarter loop. After establishing inverted flight on a 45° descending line we will begin a half slow roll. Unlike the Immelmann we will not take off all our forward stick pressure as we roll through knife edge. The first half of the maneuver is not complete until the wings are level with the airplane still on a 45° descending path of flight. After establishing this line and entry speed is again reached the second half of the maneuver will be a duplication of the first.

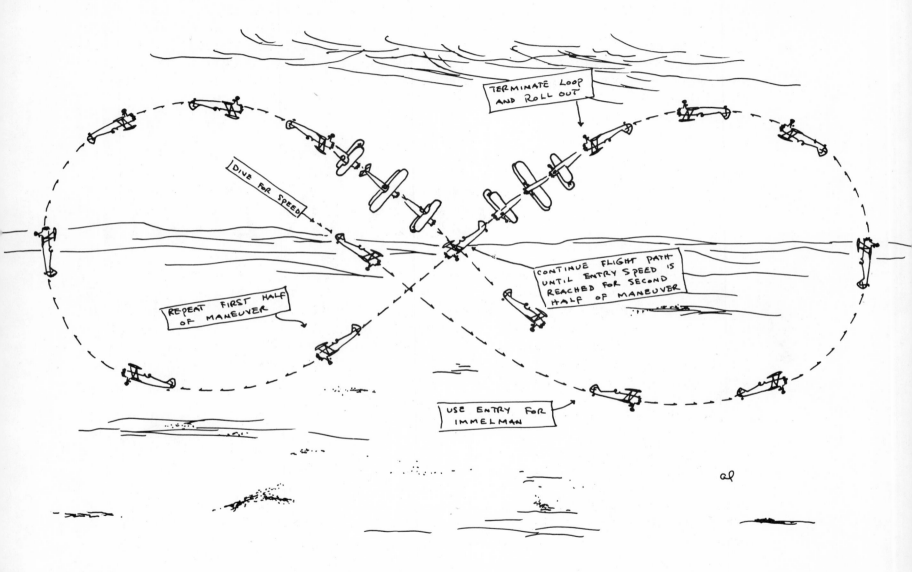

TERMINATE LOOP
AND ROLL OUT

DIVE FOR SPEED

CONTINUE FLIGHT PATH
UNTIL ENTRY SPEED IS
REACHED FOR SECOND
HALF OF MANEUVER

REPEAT FIRST HALF
OF MANEUVER

USE ENTRY FOR
IMMELMAN

CUBAN EIGHT

SLOW ROLL

On this flight we will first review Immelmanns, hammerheads and Cuban Eights, then move on to slow rolls. Since you have learned the mechanics of getting off your back by doing the half rolls out of Immelmanns and Cuban Eights, learning the slow roll will be relatively easy. From level flight we will lower the nose to pick up a 15% increase in airspeed. From there we will bring the nose up through a pre-selected point on the horizon. When the nose appears to be the same distance above the horizon as it did while flying inverted in the Immelmann we will begin application of aileron and rudder as we would a normal entry turn. However, we don't want the airplane to change its heading so at 45° of bank we will be getting off our rudder and the back pressure. As the wings approach the knife edge position the rudder and elevator will be neutral but as we pass through knife edge we will apply opposite rudder and forward elevator to coordinate the roll and hold the airplane in the same relative position with the horizon. When the airplane becomes inverted we will neutralize both the rudder and aileron to stop the roll. Holding it there momentarily you will note that your line of sight is on the point you previously passed through and the nose of the airplane is the same distance above the horizon as it was in the Immelmanns. After hesitating in the inverted position return to normal flight in precisely the same manner you used in the Immelmann. When this is accomplished you will have in reality completed a two point slow roll. We will continue the two segment roll until you have learned the mechanics of the entry, then we will put the two halves together into one smooth operation to form a slow roll.

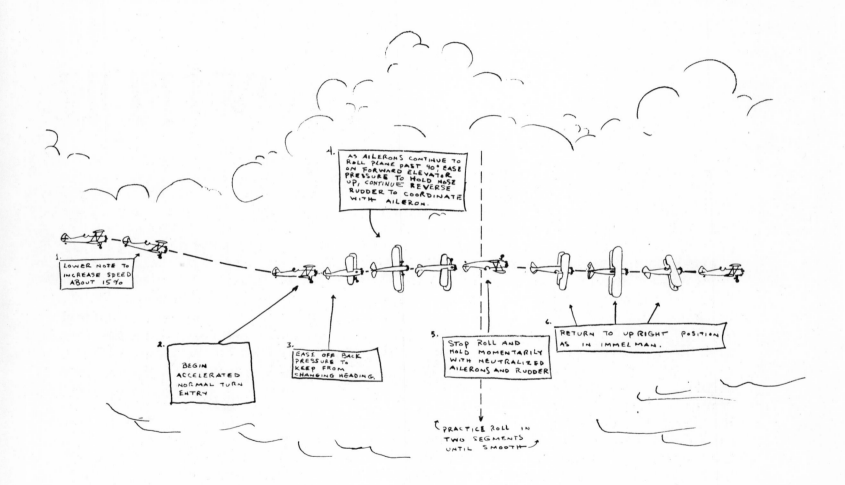

SLOW ROLL

By learning a slow roll in this manner you will never have trouble with any rolling maneuvers because you are cognizant of the control movements and pressures in any segment of the roll.

SPLIT-S

After the session with the slow rolls, we will capitalize on what you have previously learned by taking half of two maneuvers and putting them together to make another. The maneuver I am referring to is the Split-S. It consists of a half roll with a half loop recovery. Like a spin it is an altitude-losing maneuver and requires a thorough inspection of the airspace beneath the airplane before starting. Actually, it loses altitude faster than a spin. For that reason it is one of the most dangerous of all aerobatic maneuvers if started too low or not executed properly.

To do this maneuver with precision, line up over a road and using a normal slow roll entry, roll to the inverted position. When this position is reached, tilt your head back to locate the road and reduce the power to lessen the forward speed. When the airplane has decelerated to the speed you would ordinarily have in the top of a loop, reverse the elevator and complete the maneuver as you would the last half of a loop.

Later on when you begin putting together combinations of maneuvers, you will find the Split-S useful in positioning. It will give you a 180° change of direction and the speed necessary for your next maneuver.

There are two methods of entry into a Split-S. The one you have just learned, and from a half snap roll.

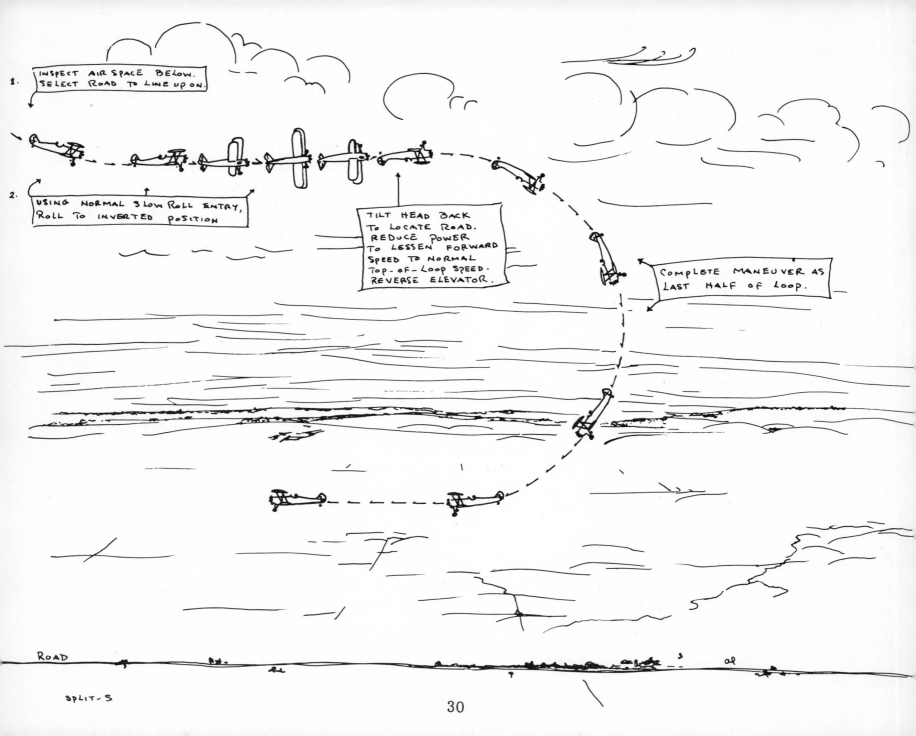

1. INSPECT AIR SPACE BELOW. SELECT ROAD TO LINE UP ON.

2. USING NORMAL SLOW ROLL ENTRY, ROLL TO INVERTED POSITION

TILT HEAD BACK TO LOCATE ROAD. REDUCE POWER TO LESSEN FORWARD SPEED TO NORMAL TOP-OF-LOOP SPEED. REVERSE ELEVATOR.

COMPLETE MANEUVER AS LAST HALF OF LOOP.

ROAD

SPLIT-S

REVERSE CUBAN EIGHT

There are many varieties of the Cuban Eight demonstrated by professional airshow pilots including outside Cuban Eights that begin in inverted flight and are terminated in the same attitude. They do them half inside and half outside or half outside and half inside but since this is a basic course we will leave the more advanced eights to the airshow people.

There is, however, one other variation of the Cuban Eight that we will cover. It is called the reverse Cuban Eight. It takes more skill than the normal Cuban Eight but once it is mastered it's a lot more fun.

From a dive to attain the same entry speed as that of an Immelmann we will bring the airplane up to a 45° ascending line. With the nose of the climbing airplane shutting off our view of the horizon we will have to establish this line by reference to the wings.

When the line has been established we will roll to the inverted position as rapidly as possible. We will hold the inverted line until it is as long as the upright line was before the roll. We will then reduce the throttle and apply back pressure as needed to complete a loop. The arc of the loop must be large enough to provide for a build up of speed equivalent to that of the original entry. Once that speed is attained we will again establish a 45° ascending line and complete the maneuver with a duplication of the first half of it.

This is one of the most difficult of all basic maneuvers to learn. Since the airplane is rapidly dissipating speed on the climbing line we must roll as fast as possible. The fast half roll also requires a rapid application of the controls to stop it. Most students have trouble with this. They go right on past the inverted position until they get the knack of stopping the roll as quickly as they started it.

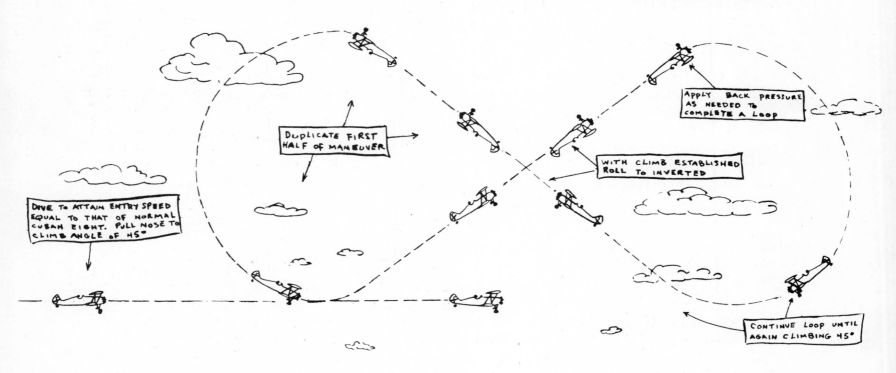

REVERSE CUBAN EIGHT

DUPLICATE FIRST HALF OF MANEUVER

APPLY BACK PRESSURE AS NEEDED TO COMPLETE A LOOP

WITH CLIMB ESTABLISHED ROLL TO INVERTED

DIVE TO ATTAIN ENTRY SPEED EQUAL TO THAT OF NORMAL CUBAN EIGHT. PULL NOSE TO CLIMB ANGLE OF 45°

CONTINUE LOOP UNTIL AGAIN CLIMBING 45°

With the airplane continuing to slow down after it is inverted, increased forward pressure is required to hold the line. Many students overdo this. As a result the airplane stalls inverted -- the nose drops and they end up making a half loop recovery from a busted maneuver. Others may not use enough forward pressure resulting in a sagging line as the nose comes down and an excessive rate of speed with the danger of high G loads in the recovery.

SQUARE LOOP

Noah Webster informs us that a loop is circular and a square is rectangular, so if one goes by the book he would not believe a square loop possible. In some airplanes it is not, but if your trainer has an inverted system it is quite possible to do the misnamed maneuver called a square loop.

Your entry speed will be as high or higher for this maneuver as any you have done. To execute the square, you must establish a horizontal line with enough speed to complete a tight 90 degree pull up, a vertical ascending line of the same length as the horizontal line, another tight 90 degree corner, and establish an inverted horizontal line that can be held as long as the others without a loss of altitude.

The third corner and the vertical descending line, forming the fourth side of the square, pose no such problem. In fact, the throttle must be retarded as soon as the down line is established to prevent over-speeding.

A square drawn on a piece of paper is completed when the line forming the fourth side intersects the line forming the first side. However, this is not true when flying a square. The maneuver is not finished until the fourth corner is completed with the airplane in normal level flight along the first line. To get a good sharp fourth corner, the throttle should be opened as back pressure is applied to bring the nose up. This will provide a greater flow of air over the elevator and consequently a more effective elevator.

Some instructors teach their students to keep their lines equal by counting. Such a procedure is perfectly all right, but remember this makes them equal in time only. Variance in airspeed will vary the length of lines relative to the body of air you are flying in; wind conditions will vary them relative to the ground over which you are flying. Airshow pilots make the bottom line into the wind. Thus, the inverted airplane slowed down on the top line has the advantage of the tail wind to help make the lines appear to be the same length.

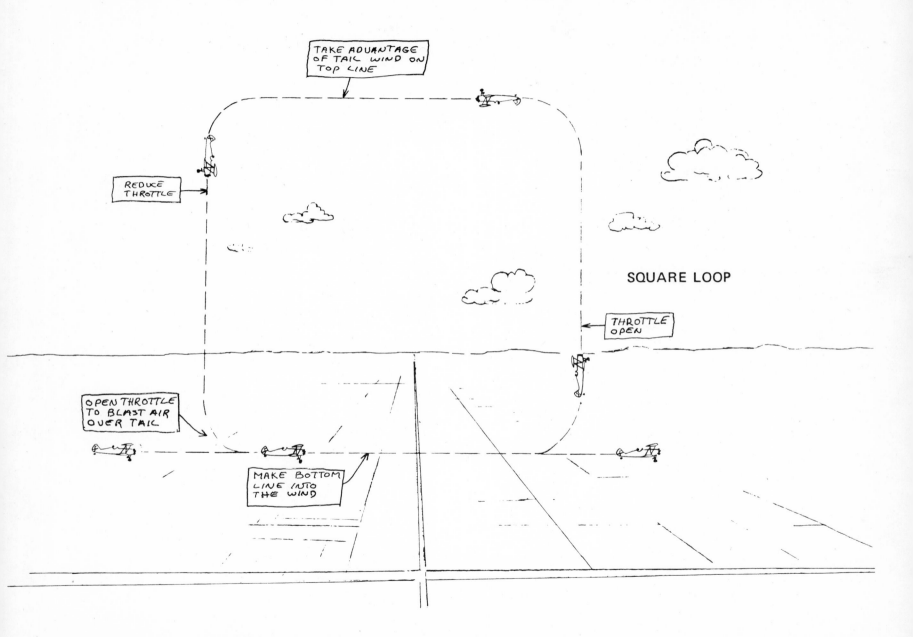

35

SNAP ROLLS

As we move on to snap roll maneuvers, you will acquire a different concept of control movements. Visualize the snap roll as a spin on the horizontal plane. The spin and the snap roll are both started with a stall, but in a different manner. Control movements in the spin entry are used to direct the course of the airplane as it approaches the power-off stall. In snap rolls, the controls serve a like purpose, but in addition are used to induce a high speed stall with full power on.

We have discussed before the fact that in level flight the cowling appears to be below the line of the horizon. To enter a snap roll, bring the nose up with back pressure. As it crosses the horizon, open the throttle and increase the back pressure with an abrupt pull and simultaneously use an abrupt application of rudder in the direction you wish to roll. The sharp change in the angle of attack caused by the excessive back pressure, in turn, causes a high speed stall. As the stall breaks, (snaps -- this may be the origination of the name) the positive use of rudder motivates the roll. To get a more rapid rate of roll and to dampen the oscillation of the nose, apply full aileron in the direction of the roll as the stick reaches its most rearward position. The airplane will continue rolling as long as it is held in the stall. However, when the forward momentum is lost, the roll will progress into a power spin.

For a one turn snap, start the recovery about three quarters of the way around. Neutralize the ailerons and release the back pressure and at the same time reverse the rudder to the full opposite position. It is usually beneficial to use opposite aileron to aid in slowing down the rate of roll. As the wings approach the level position, snap the stick forward to return the airplane to its original attitude and neutralize the aileron and rudder. I usually leave the throttle full forward until I start recovery, then ease it back to cruising rpm as the rotation stops.

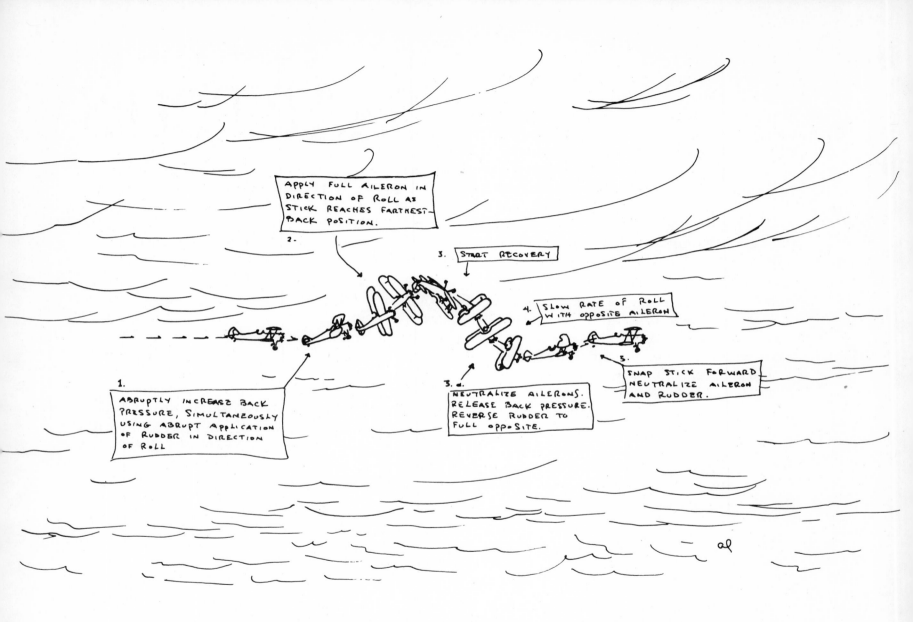

APPLY FULL AILERON IN
DIRECTION OF ROLL AS
STICK REACHES FARTHEST
BACK POSITION.
2.

3. START RECOVERY

4. SLOW RATE OF ROLL
WITH OPPOSITE AILERON

1.
ABRUPTLY INCREASE BACK
PRESSURE, SIMULTANEOUSLY
USING ABRUPT APPLICATION
OF RUDDER IN DIRECTION
OF ROLL

3. a.
NEUTRALIZE AILERONS.
RELEASE BACK PRESSURE.
REVERSE RUDDER TO
FULL OPPOSITE.

5.
SNAP STICK FORWARD
NEUTRALIZE AILERON
AND RUDDER.

SNAP ROLL

Half snap rolls are started in the same manner as full snap rolls, but there the similarity ends. For one thing, you have to think and react much faster. From the time the stall breaks until you have rotated 60° is probably less than a second. But it is at this point you must begin your recovery. The recovery is accomplished by a very positive reversal of all the controls. As the rotation stops, the rudder and aileron must be neutralized immediately.

There are two practical recoveries from the half snap roll. Either a half slow roll, or a Split-S will get you back to the right side up position. Naturally, the simplest way to recover from a half snap is by using a Split-S. Since the half snap roll is completed at only a little over stalling speed, all you have to do is make sure the wings are level before starting the Split-S.

A one and a half turn snap roll is not a difficult maneuver to learn after you have mastered the one half and full snap rolls. Certainly, there is an orientation problem, but the elapsed time of the maneuver makes planning and timing the recovery much easier. Excess speed will be necessary to keep the airplane rolling on the horizontal plane. In most airplanes, it is advantageous to lower the nose to increase speed before starting the pull up. This maneuver, as all others we have covered, is to be executed only in an aerobatic trainer approved for multiple snap rolls. Snap rolls produce, momentarily, a high G load. The faster the entry speed, the greater the load. Since the heavy G load is sustained only momentarily, you can probably get by with one snap roll at any speed. However, one snap roll at speeds higher than recommended may weaken the structure of the airplane and each succeeding one adds to the weakness. If this abusive practice continues, failure of the weakened part is bound to occur.

Someone is forever asking me what is the best snap rolling airplanes. I have not flown all the aerobatic airplanes, but I can say one thing for sure, it is not the clipped wing Taylorcraft. From many years of observation I would have to say the best snap rolling airplane of all time is Curtis Pitts' wonderful little Pitts Special. The way present day airshow pilots snap this airplane is a thing of

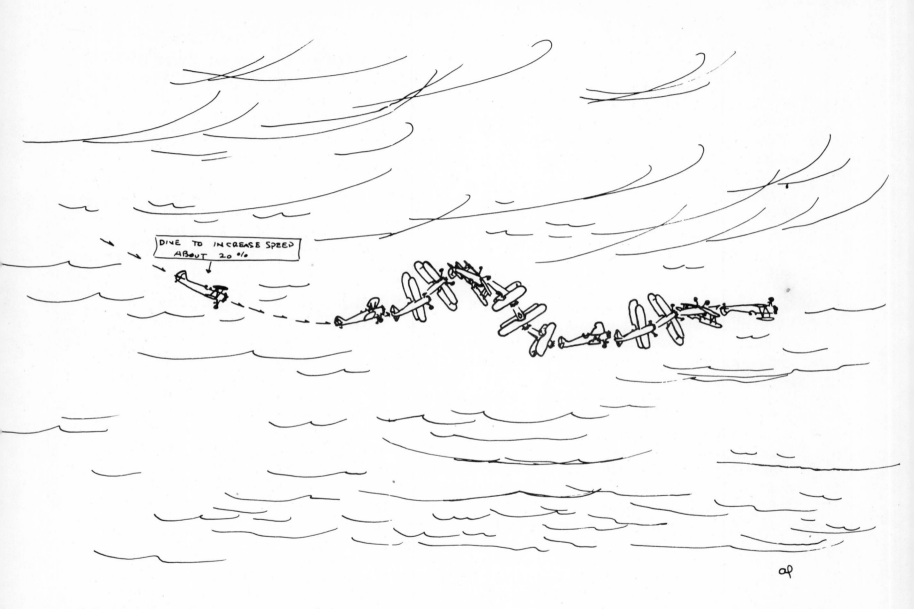

SNAP-and-A-HALF

beauty. They execute single, double, triple and quadruple snap rolls. They do them from right side up to inverted, from inverted to right side up, to knife edge and from knife edge, inside and outside -- it does not seem to matter from what position they start or in what position they end up. Their recoveries are always on the point and with speed enough to continue in normal flight.

We will continue working on snap maneuvers with a snap roll in the top of a loop. Understandably, the maneuver will require more speed than a simple country loop (as my brother Arnold calls them). Using the speed required for an Immelman, begin the loop. When you have completed approximately 150° of the loop, increase the back pressure sharply and apply rudder and aileron as you would in a normal snap roll. At approximately three quarters of the rotation, make a normal snap roll recovery paying special attention to use of elevator. The nose must stop on the original perimeter of the loop. Starting the snap too soon will produce a nose-high recovery resulting in falling back into the orbit of the loop. If the snap is begun too late, the recovery will be made farther down on the last half of the loop than it was started on the first half. True symmetry of this maneuver is difficult to accomplish.

SNAP ROLL AT TOP OF LOOP

42

SLOW ROLL ON THE TOP OF A LOOP

We will begin our loop with the same speed we would use in an Immelmann. We will begin the roll at the same point we began the snap in the snap roll on the top of a loop. The roll is started in the usual manner, but after 90 degrees of rotation the amount of elevator pressure does not correspond to that used in a slow roll on a horizontal plane. It is true that elevator pressure is important in maintaining the vertical flight path, but since the point on which you are rolling is following the arc of the loop, less forward pressure is needed to hold that point. In a properly planned maneuver, the airplane should have rotated 180° at the apogee of the loop. In the last half of the roll, rudder and aileron pressure are used in the same manner as in a horizontal roll, but once again, the elevator pressure, though applied in the same manner, is done so in a lesser degree to hold the ever-changing point on the perimeter of the loop.

After an introduction to the slow roll in the top of a loop, you will agree that because of the difficulty in holding a point over such a wide arc of the loop that a considerable amount of practicing will be needed to perfect the maneuver. Airplanes are suited to different maneuvers. An excellent example of this can be seen by comparing a Stearman with a midget racer in the execution of the slow roll at the top of a loop. For instance, Steve Wittman or Bob Downey do them with perfect precision. As a result of the tremendous speed of their midget racers, the circumference of their loop is correspondingly large and with their rapid rate of roll, the length of the arc they traverse in the roll is correspondingly short.

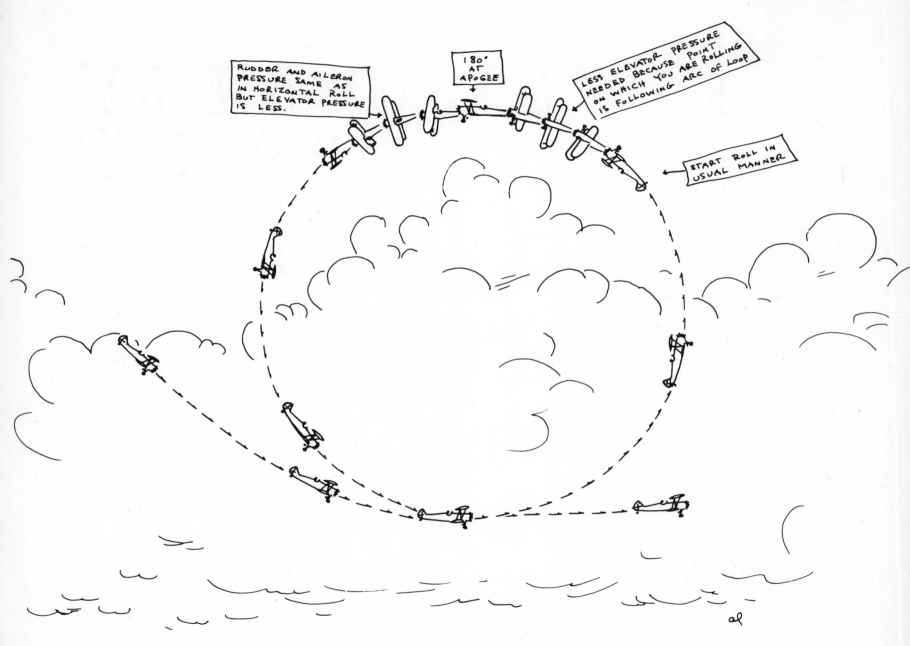

SLOW ROLL AT TOP OF LOOP

44

BARREL ROLL

By comparison, the control movements in a barrel roll are much simpler than those used in a slow roll. As a result of this simplicity, habits may be developed that are hard to overcome. Therein lies the reason for teaching this maneuver late in the course.

We will begin the maneuver by selecting a point on the horizon 20 degrees to one side or the other of straight ahead about which to roll, then let the nose down to gain entry speed. When the same speed is reached as that used in a slow roll, we will initiate a pull up and as the nose crosses the horizon, continue the back pressure while beginning a coordinated application of rudder and aileron in the desired direction of rotation. After rotating the first 45 degrees, we will ease off the rudder but continue the use of aileron and back pressure until the first quarter of the roll is completed. At this point the wings are perpendicular to the horizon, the airplane is at its highest position in the roll, and is directly above the point around which it is rolling. With continued aileron pressure, we will decrease back pressure at the rate necessary to remove all of it by the time the airplane has rotated 180 degrees and rolled to the inverted position. By continuing the use of aileron only, the airplane will rotate 270 degrees and be directly below the point around which it is rolling with the wings again perpendicular to the horizon in the second knife edge position. From this attitude, left rudder and elevator are applied once more to complete the roll on its original heading with the nose back up in its proper perspective to the horizon.

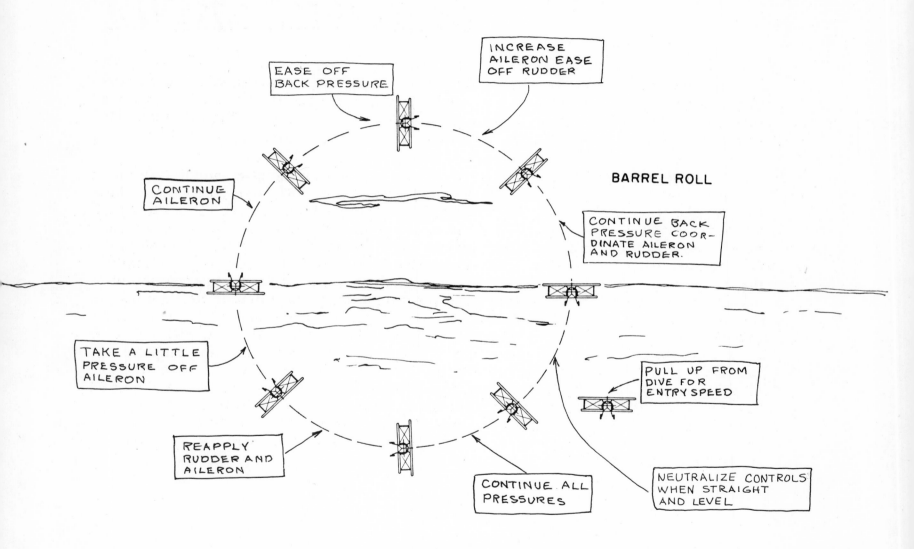

BARREL ROLL

EASE OFF BACK PRESSURE

INCREASE AILERON EASE OFF RUDDER

CONTINUE AILERON

CONTINUE BACK PRESSURE COOR- DINATE AILERON AND RUDDER.

TAKE A LITTLE PRESSURE OFF AILERON

PULL UP FROM DIVE FOR ENTRY SPEED

REAPPLY RUDDER AND AILERON

CONTINUE ALL PRESSURES

NEUTRALIZE CONTROLS WHEN STRAIGHT AND LEVEL

INVERTED TURNS

You will most likely become disoriented during the introduction of inverted turns. The sky below and the ground above as the nose swings around in the turn is an unnatural situation that takes some getting used to. Then too, you are hanging on the belt which is not the most comfortable seating arrangement. However, you will soon adjust to the upside down world and become accustomed to the discomfort of sitting on your lap. To help with this and to learn inverted coordination we will do a series of two point slow rolls with about a half minute inverted flight between the two halves of the roll.

When you have sufficiently mastered straight and level inverted flight we will move on to the inverted turn. After rolling the airplane to the upside down position we will apply aileron with opposite rudder to coordinate the entry and add forward pressure to compensate for loss of lift due to the bank. Then, as in a normal turn, once it is established, we will neutralize the rudder and bring the aileron back against the bank to keep it from getting steeper.

If during the turn a wing drops or raises, increasing or decreasing the bank, a coordinated correction is used and this means the use of aileron and opposite rudder. These corrections will give you a sensation of flying with crossed controls, but since you have been schooled in the use of aileron and rudder in inverted flight, it won't be long before it will become natural to use them properly while in inverted turns.

Holding the nose in its proper attitude with respect to the horizon seems to be the most common problem. If you get the nose too high from excessive forward pressure, most likely the bank will increase and the airplane will roll upright before the turn is completed. This is no big thing but if you let the nose get down because of a lack of forward pressure, you could be headed for trouble. If this happens, roll back to right-side-up flight.

90 DEGREE INVERTED TURN

Use of controls in 90 degree inverted turn. At point A begin coordination of left aileron and right rudder and increase forward pressure. As turn and bank are established at point B, neutralize rudder and apply aileron against bank to prevent over banking. At point C begin roll out by coordinating right aileron and left rudder. At point D neutralize aileron and rudder and reduce forward pressure.

SLOW ROLL IN A 90° TURN

In my opinion, there are five basic aerobatic maneuvers -- loops, slow rolls, snap rolls, inverted flight, and vertical flight. All others are combinations of or parts of the five basic maneuvers.

Unless we learn the five basics well, the combinations will become progressively more difficult. In high school, I used to skip school to go fishing or to hitch-hike to the Mt. Hawley Airport in Peoria. I was a fair football player, so my grades automatically stayed at the passing level. That is, with the exception of geometry. My math teacher was so interested in school that she did not care whether football kept or not. Geometry is learned by progressive steps. Consequently, every time I missed a class I continued to flunk until I had gone back and learned the lesson I had missed. If you do not master the basic maneuvers in aerobatics, you will not flunk, but you will spend countless costly hours, in both time and money, trying to perfect maneuvers that should be relatively easy. With this in mind it is important to continue reviewing the basics throughout your training.

The importance of knowing the fundamentals will never be more obvious than while learning a slow roll in a 90° turn. It is an extremely difficult maneuver to do well because the roll is made around an ever changing point.

If it is perfectly executed, the wings will pass through the knife edge position as the turning nose reaches a point 22.5 degrees from straight ahead. When the nose has turned 45 degrees, the wings will be in the inverted attitude. After 67.5

degrees of turning, the wings will be passing through the last knife edge position. Continuing with a constant rate of turn and roll, the airplane will attain level flight on a heading 90 degrees from where it started.

The maneuver is begun with the same entry speed as a conventional slow roll. However, after the dive for speed the nose of the airplane is brought up only as far as the horizon before the roll is started. At this time left aileron and rudder are coordinated as in a normal turn with an excess of back pressure to bring the nose up. It will reach its highest attitude at knife edge and remain there as the ailerons rotate the airplane through inverted flight and back to the second knife edge position. During this period of rotation, the airplane is turned by the use of rudder. In this instance, however, to use the verb turned is to use it rather loosely. Really, the nose of the airplane is virtually dragged around the middle 45 degrees of the maneuver by extreme use of right rudder.

For the last quarter of the rolling turn, left rudder is again coordinated with left aileron while forward stick pressure is increased to lower the nose from its high attitude to normal flight 90 degrees from the original heading.

The most common error in this maneuver is to roll out before turning 90 degrees. This usually is the result of insufficient rudder between the two knife edge positions or too little elevator from straight and level to the first knife edge position or from the second knife edge position back to normal level flight.

Four slow rolls in a 360 degree turn is, of course, just a matter of putting four ninety degree rolls together in one continuous maneuver.

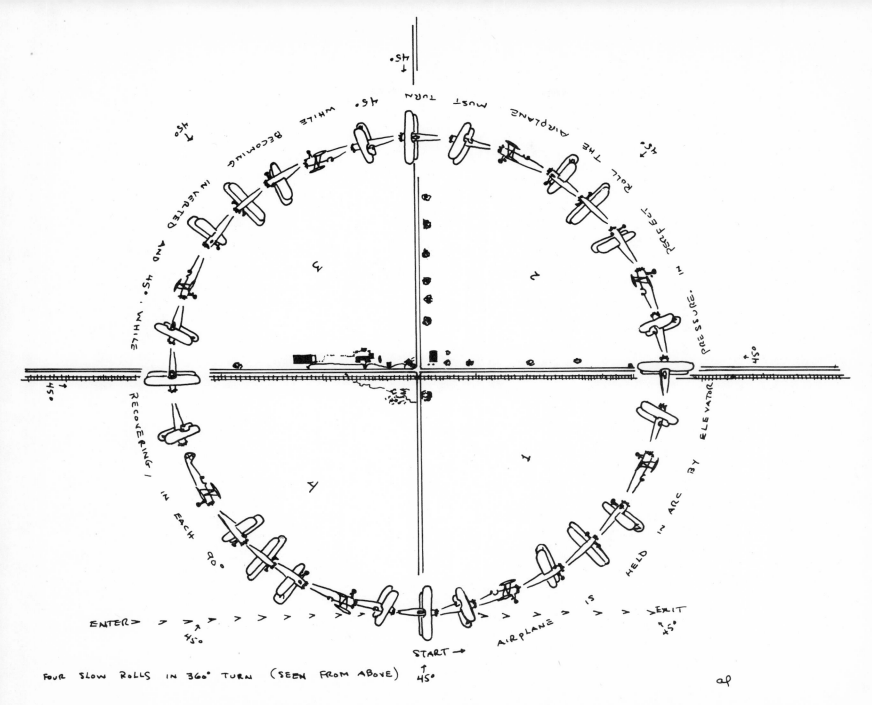

FOUR SLOW ROLLS IN 360° TURN (SEEN FROM ABOVE)

VERTICAL QUARTER SLOW ROLL

Most trainers are not capable of full vertical slow rolls, but I know of none that can't perform at least a quarter vertical slow roll so I have included the maneuver in my ten hour aerobatic course.

Lined up over a road we will begin the maneuver as any hammerhead except for entry speed. This one will require at least as high an entry speed as an Immelmann. As soon as a good vertical line is established apply aileron. Since the vertical roll is a true aileron roll the rudder is used only to keep the nose from veering off the vertical line and the elevator to prevent any movement about the lateral axis. When the airplane has rotated 90° the wings will be aligned parallel to the road over which you made the entry. At the termination of the quarter roll neutralize the aileron and enter a left hammerhead stall for recovery to level flight.

On becoming proficient in the vertical quarter roll we will add a descending quarter roll. At the completion of the stall we will pick a point on the ground for reference and roll around it. Again I want to caution you concerning the rapid build up of speed with the nose down. However, by beginning the roll as soon as the vertical down line is established and making the recovery as soon as practical after the roll is completed there should be no danger. If, during the recovery of this maneuver, or any other, the airplane should exceed its maximum recommended speed, do not panic and haul back on the stick. Speed in itself poses little danger, but violent or erratic maneuvering at excessive speed imposes G loads proportionately greater than like maneuvering at reduced speed. Recovery can be made safely by smooth, positive application of back pressure while keeping the airplane straight with aileron and rudder.

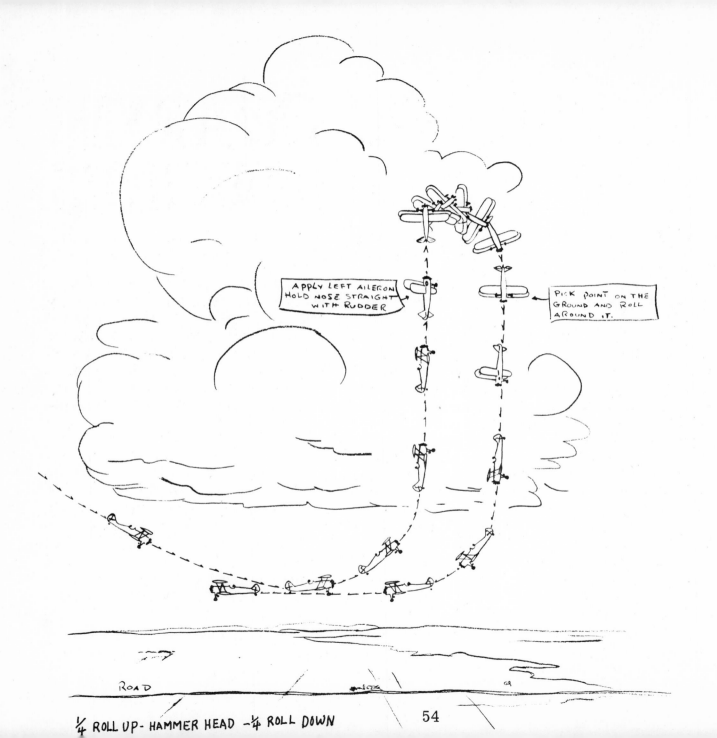

APPLY LEFT AILERON
HOLD NOSE STRAIGHT
WITH RUDDER

PICK POINT ON THE
GROUND AND ROLL
AROUND IT.

ROAD

¼ ROLL UP- HAMMER HEAD -¼ ROLL DOWN

54

A NEW LOOK
AT AEROBATICS

Through my very able illustrator, Alice Eakles Marks, I have been able to diagram the maneuvers while showing you the various positions of the aircraft as it traverses the diagrams. For obvious reasons, this sort of illustration is a very necessary component of the book, but as we progress, we need a simpler system of illustration. In this period, we will be putting the maneuvers we have learned together in sequences. To help you keep the maneuvers in their proper order, we will use the system of diagraming designed by Count Jose L. Aresti of Spain. This unique system is used for diagraming the routines of all national and international aerobatic competitors.

Any maneuver or combinations of maneuvers can be diagramed by using the key to Aresti's aerial figures.

BASIC KEYS

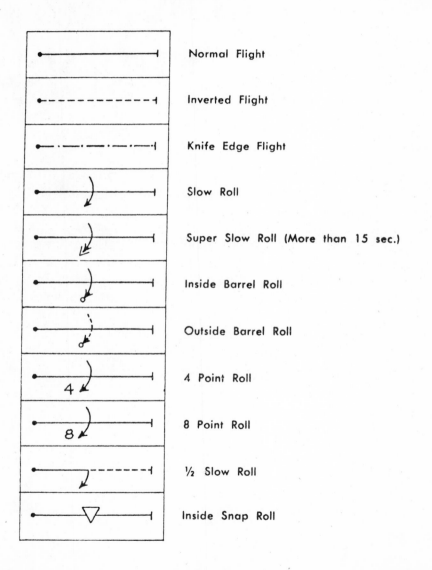

	Normal Flight
	Inverted Flight
	Knife Edge Flight
	Slow Roll
	Super Slow Roll (More than 15 sec.)
	Inside Barrel Roll
	Outside Barrel Roll
	4 Point Roll
	8 Point Roll
	½ Slow Roll
	Inside Snap Roll

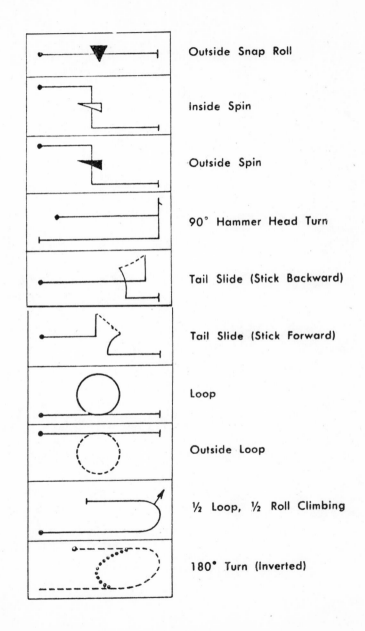

Outside Snap Roll

Inside Spin

Outside Spin

90° Hammer Head Turn

Tail Slide (Stick Backward)

Tail Slide (Stick Forward)

Loop

Outside Loop

½ Loop, ½ Roll Climbing

180° Turn (Inverted)

AEROBATICS IN SEQUENCE

After completing a dual aerobatic course consisting of the basic maneuvers you will want to start putting them together in sequences. To help you with this we will diagram a couple of sequences for you to practice and tape them to the instrument panel. They should be placed as near eye level as possible without covering up any of the instruments. While flying an airshow, I like to think of the aerobatic area as a giant theatre with that area directly in front of the spectators as the stage and the turn around areas as the wings. By properly planning my routine with positioning maneuvers done in the wings, I have no trouble holding my position in the center of the stage. To aid you in holding your position, we have diagramed the practice sequences with the same thought in mind.

In the past, you completed only one maneuver before regaining the lost altitude so it was safe enough to start at 3,000 feet, but now that you are going to do a series of maneuvers without stopping, begin the maneuvering at 4,000 feet.

The first sequence will begin with a half snap roll to the inverted position. From that position, do a Split-S. Coming out of the Split-S, enter a loop. From the completed loop, execute a hammerhead stall to get back into position and to provide enough speed to finish the sequence with a snap roll in the top of a loop.

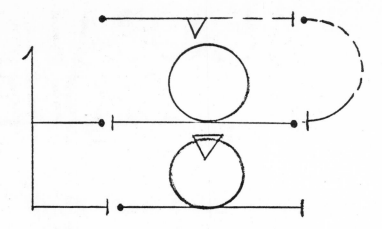

The second set of maneuvers will begin with a slow roll to the left followed by a right half slow roll to the inverted position. Once again, use a Split-S to get turned around. Plan to recover from the Split-S with enough speed to enter the fourth maneuver, a Cuban eight. A hammerhead stall subsequent to the Cuban eight will give you speed and position for an Immelman, the final maneuver.

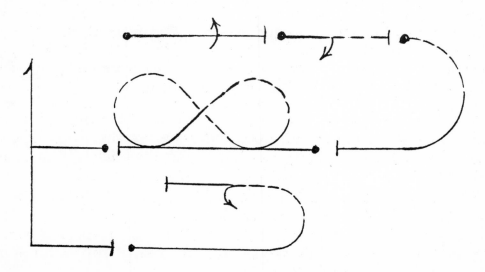

Military flying cadets are taught that man was given a neck to be used as a swivel to turn his head on. In the World War II training days, we graded a student down as much for not looking around as we did for poor flying. In preparing these youngsters for combat, we were teaching them a means of self preservation. In combat, if they were to live to fight another day, they had to see their enemy before he saw them. Now we don't have to worry about Zeros or Folke Wolfes, but in this day of head in the cockpit flying and areas of high density traffic, we have enemies just as deadly. Witness the great number of mid-airs and near misses of the past few years. In each instance, someone was negligent. This sort of negligence on the part of a pilot makes him the enemy of everyone who flys.

An aerobatic pilot learns to fly with his head out of the cockpit. He must be cognizant of his position relative to the ground, the attitude of his airplane relative to the horizon, and, above all, the position of any traffic in the area. The division of attention required to fly a sequence of maneuvers is invaluable in strengthening your perceptibility, and as a result, enhances your chances of survival in this era of hurrying and scurrying whether you are flying, driving, or even walking.

Laying out a planned routine is a good habit to get into for reasons other than positioning. Planned practice periods save time and money. Wandering around the sky wondering what to do next is costly.

If you bungle a maneuver while practicing a sequence, break off and start over again. While climbing back to altitude you will have time to reflect on your error and once again be at a safe altitude to complete the sequence.

DO'S AND DON'TS

After completing ten hours of dual instruction, you will have acquired confidence in the airplane and yourself. As a natural result of the course, you will have eliminated any misgivings or apprehensions you may have had and improved all phases of your flying proficiency by gaining a greater knowledge of the controls and their functions. You will realize that you are not a qualified aerobatic pilot, but that you do have a solid background on which to continue if you wish to do so. To become a polished aerobatic pilot takes hours and hours of practice.

I have found in business dealings that the fellow who boasts of his honesty is probably a crook. So it is with the braggart who extols his ability as an aerobatic pilot. If he is good, he does not need to brag. I have never heard a top-notch airshow pilot crow about his ability. These fellows know that one never completely masters the art of aerobatic flying. I have been doing aerobatics as an instructor, for my own personal pleasure, and professionally for thirty-six years and I am still learning. My brothers, Marion and Lester, started in this business of aerobatics after I did, yet I have learned a lot from them. I have gained an immeasurable amount of knowledge from watching and listening to my competitors. My son Rolly and I coached each other while practicing for competitive events and though he had been flying aerobatics for only a few short years, he taught me a lot. People are prone to credit me with Rolly's greatness, but this is wrong. Like all great aerobatic pilots, he got there by hard work. Not a day passed in the four months he owned the 450 Stearman that he did not practice if weather conditions permitted.

Confirmation of the need for practice can be found by anyone arriving at the site of a National Championship Aerobatic contest a week early. They will find the practice area filled with the nation's finest aerobatic pilots practicing to make themselves better.

If you do not own an aerobatic airplane and want to continue your training, you will have one of two alternatives -- either to buy or to rent. In either event, be doubly sure you are dealing with a reputable operator. DO NOT fly aerobatics in every Tom, Dick, and Harry's airplane.

It seems that everywhere I go someone wants me to fly their home-built. "Wring it out", they say. I do not like the phrase, but even if I did, I would still refuse to fly their airplane. As a chain is only as strong as its weakest link, an airplane is only as strong as its weakest point (welds, fittings, spars, longerons, engine mounts, etc.). To fly aerobatics in an airplane of unknown quality is to invite trouble. This warning pertains to manufactured airplanes as well as home-builts.

Even if you rent an aircraft from a reputable operator, check the operations manual and the log books for recent inspections and repairs. NEVER fly aerobatics in any airplane without first giving it a good visual inspection. Check every fitting, bolt, or weld that you can see. Remove enough wing inspection plates to check the drag and anti-drag wires. Any looseness indicates that something in the wing has moved. Check for wrinkles in the skin or fabric. A wrinkle is usually an indication of structural breakdown.

If you own the airplane, always wash it yourself and include washing down the engine. Washing the airplane presents the best opportunity I know of to inspect the airplane and to keep current on its condition.

If you do not own an airplane, but plan to buy one, DO NOT take the seller's word as to its condition. Insist on a one hundred hour inspection by a mechanic of your choice. Remember, your life may depend on the airworthiness of the airplane.

You may find an unairworthy airplane that you wish to buy and rebuild. There is nothing wrong with this thinking. By having an airplane rebuilt or doing it yourself, you can at least be sure of the airframe. However, you can still run into trouble. The FAA does its best to prevent malfunctions of engine mounts, engines, propellers, etc. by its demand for rigid inspections. But with all its rules and regulations, it cannot govern human behavior. Bogus components are occasionally sold -- some by error and some unscrupulously. Before you buy any major component, make a thorough check of the integrity of the manufacturer or overhaul station you intend to patronize. Take this advise from a grieving father who lost a son due to a malfunction.

Now I have another don't for you. <u>DON'T</u> show off. -- I learned this the hard way a long time ago. In those days pilots were called aviators, and, as such, they were understandably local heroes. We lesser pilots admired their ability and bragged to all and sundry that they were our instructors or friends. I looked forward to the day when others would admire my flying and talk about me with the same reverence they did the older pilots.

One day, I decided the time had come to show my contemporaries what a hot pilot I was. Swaggering over to a Taylor Cub, I asked with a 'mightier than thou' attitude, "How about one of you guys giving me a crank?" As I taxied out, I felt that I had already made a favorable impression. I took the Cub up to about 1500 feet and after doing a couple of loops I was certain that my audience was marveling at my superb flying. However, I was not satisfied. I wanted to prove my superiority with a spectacular finale. I had seen the old-timers buzz the runway downwind, then pull up in a wing over to land going into the wind. This was for me. Such a stunt would be a real clincher.

I came down the runway wide open (75 miles per hour) not over ten feet above the ground and started my pull-up about 200 feet in front of my friends. I knew the higher I made the pull-up the more spectacular the maneuver would be, so once I got the nose pointed up, I held it there. I held it until I suddenly realized the controls were getting soft. I don't recall how I got the airplane turned around and headed down, but I do recall how fast the ground was coming up and how useless the elevator seemed. When the elevator did take effect, I brought the nose up, but continued mushing downward. Just missing the ground by inches I pulled up to reflect on my stupidity.

Had I made the the recovery a second later it might have been the end of my life.

COMPETITIVE AEROBATICS

Competitive aerobatics become more popular each year due to the efforts of the International Aerobatic Club, a division of the Experimental Aircraft Association. Dedicated to grass roots aerobatics, they encourage the sport by sanctioning aerobatic contests throughout United States and Canada. Usually about the first week in August they hold the International Aerobatic Championships in Fond du Lac, Wisconsin.

To cover all stages of development in pilots and capabilities of aerobatic planes the contests are divided into four categories -- Sportsman, Intermediate, Advanced, and Unlimited. Pilots in the Sportsman class fly only a known compulsory sequence of maneuvers. Intermediate pilots fly both a compulsory group of figures and a free style sequence of their own choosing. In the Advanced and Unlimited classes the contestants must fly both a known compulsory group which they have practiced and an unknown sequence of maneuvers issued the night before they are to perform them with no practice, and a free style of their own choosing. In addition, Unlimited pilots are given four minutes to present an air show routine.

To give you an insight into the quality of flying taking place at an IAC sanctioned contest and the levels of skill required to participate in each class, the next few pages are devoted to the known compulsory sequences of the 1976 aerobatic season.

SPORTSMAN SEQUENCE

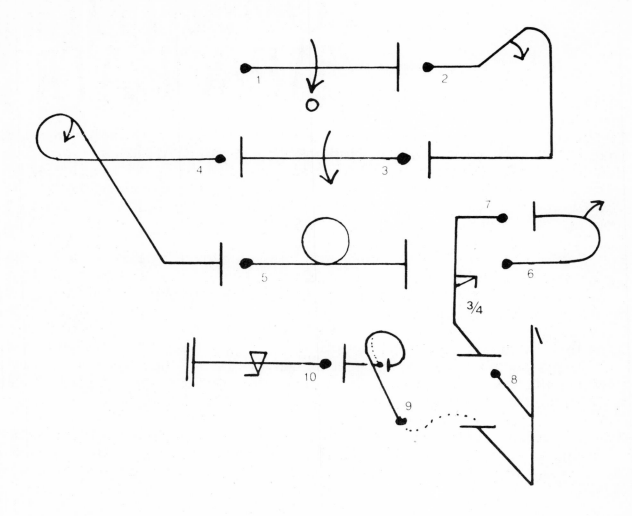

Man. No.	Aresti Number	Description	
1	8.1.2.3.1.	Inside Barrel Roll	10
2	9.2.1.2.1.	Half roll, 5/8 Loop	18
3	8.1.1.1.1.	Slow Roll	10
4	9.1.1.2.	5/8 Loop, Half Roll	16
5	7.1.1.	Loop — Inside	12
6	9.1.1.1.	Half Loop, Half Roll	17
7	4.1.2.	3/4 Inside Spin	7
8	5.1.1.	Hammerhead	20
9	2.2.	270° Turn	3
10	8.3.1.1.1.	Inside Snap Roll	10
		TOTAL	123

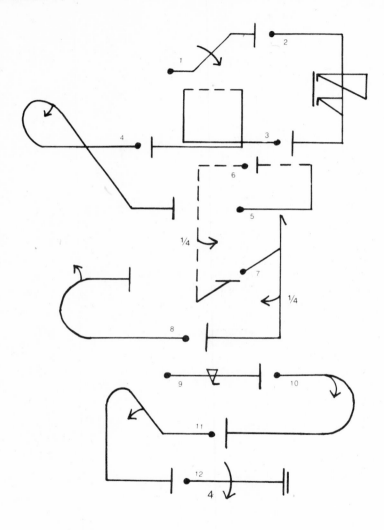

INTERMEDIATE

Man. No.	Aresti Number	Description	
1	8.1.1.6.1.	Slow Roll on 45° Up Line	16
2	4.1.7.	1-1/2 Inside Spin	12
3	7.2.1.	Inside Square Loop	18
4	9.1.1.2.	5/8 Loop, Half Roll	16
5	7.2.2.	Half Square Loop	12
6	8.1.1.11.4.3.	1/4 Roll on 90° Down Line	18
7	5.1.3.4. plus 8.1.1.5.4.	Hammerhead with 1/4 Roll Down	26
8	9.1.1.1.	Half Loop, Half Roll	17
9	8.3.1.1.1.	Inside Snap Roll	10
10	9.2.1.1.	Half Roll, Half Loop	17
11	9.2.1.2.1.	Half Roll, Half Loop	18
12	8.2.2.1.1.	4 point Slow Roll	11
		TOTAL	191

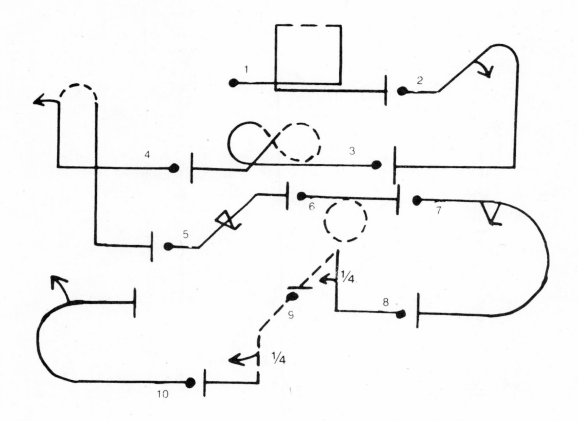

(Steps 11 thru 15 on page 73)

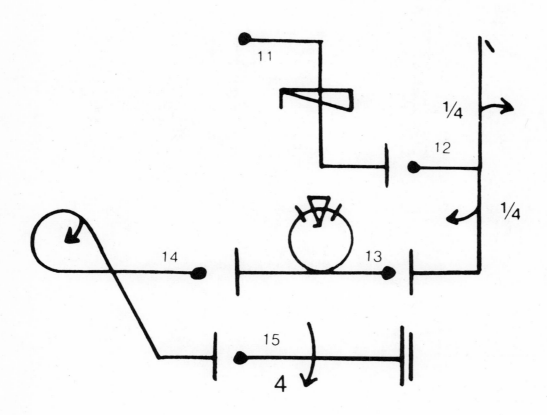

ADVANCED SEQUENCE

Man. No.	Aresti Number	Description	
1	7.2.1.	Inside Square Loop	18
2	9.2.1.2.1	Half Roll, Half Loop	18
3	7.6.1.1.	Horizontal Eight	28
4	9.2.1.4.1.	Vertical Half Roll, Push Over	27
5	8.3.1.6.1.	Inside Snap Roll on 45° Up Line	16
6	7.1.1.2.	Outside Loop from Top Down	24
7	9.2.8.1.	Half Inside Snap, Half Loop	17
8	8.1.1.10.4.2.	Quarter Vertical Roll, Push Over to Inverted	18
9	8.1.1.11.4.3.	Quarter Vertical Roll on Down Line from Inverted	18
10	9.1.1.1.	Half Loop, Half Roll	17
11	4.1.1.	Inside Spin	10
12	5.1.7.4 plus 8.1.1.4.4. plus 8.1.1.5.4.	Hammerhead with Quarter Rolls on Up and Down Lines	32
13	7.1.1. plus 8.3.1.1.1.	Snap Roll on Top of Loop	22
14	9.1.1.2.	5/8 Loop, Half Roll	16
15	8.2.2.1.1.	4-Point Roll	11
		TOTAL	292

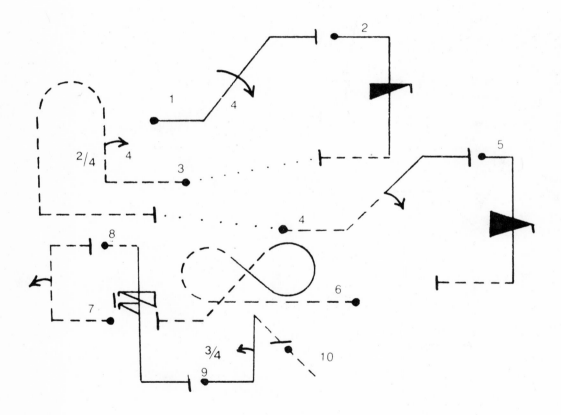

(Steps 11 thru 18 on page 76)

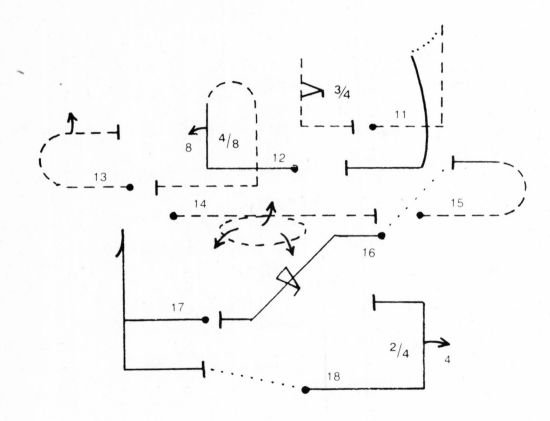

Man. No.	Aresti Number	Description	
1	8.2.2.6.1.	4 point Roll on 45 Line	17
2	4.2.1.2.	Inverted Spin-Upright Entry, Inverted Recovery	25
3	9.2.5.3.1.1.	2/4 of 4-point Vertical Roll from Inverted, Push Over, Inverted Recovery	37
4	8.1.1.6.3.2.	Half Roll on 45 Line	19
5	8.3.2.11.1.2.	Outside Snap Roll on Vertical Line, Inverted Recovery	37
6	7.6.1.1.1.	Horizontal Eight	34
7	8.1.1.10.3.1.	Vertical Half Roll from Inverted, Pull Over	26
8	4.1.7.3.	1-1/2 Inside Spin from Inverted, Upright Recovery	19
9	8.1.1.10.3.2.	3/4 Vertical Roll, Pull Over to Inverted	23
10	8.3.1.11.3.1.	3/4 Inside Snap Roll on Vertical Down Line, Inverted Recovery	26
11	6.2.3.	Stick Forward Tailslide	24
12	9.2.6.4.2.	4/8 of 8 point Vertical Roll, Push Over, Inverted Recovery	33
13	9.1.1.1.1.	Half Outside Loop, Half Roll	27
14	8.4.2.6.1.	Rolling Turn with 3 Rolls to the Outside	40
15	7.1.2.1.	Half Outside Loop	14
16	8.3.1.7.1.	Inside Snap Roll on 45 Line	16
17	5.1.1.	Hammerhead	20
18	8.2.2.10.3.	2/4 of 4-point Vertical Roll	21
		TOTAL	458

LIST OF FIGURES AND COEFFICIENTS

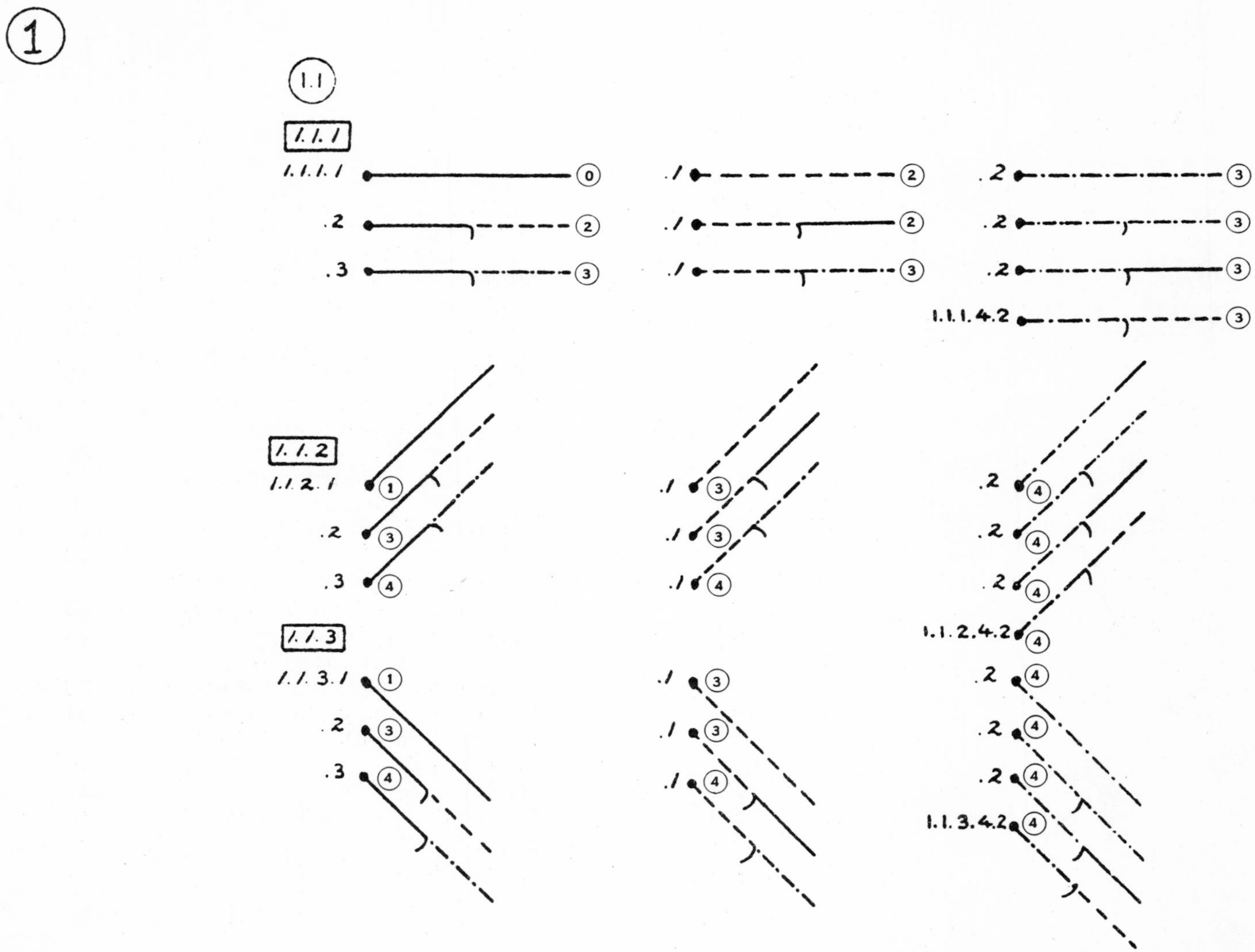

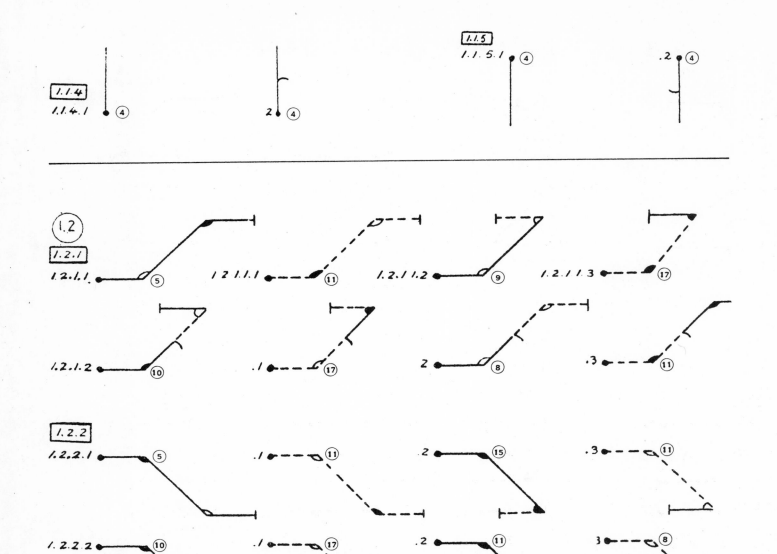

79

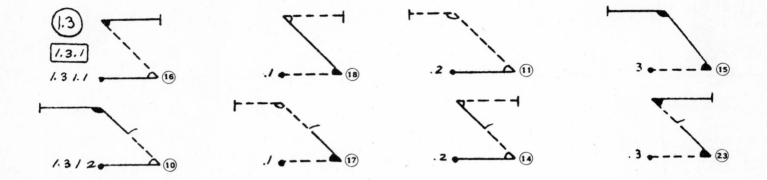

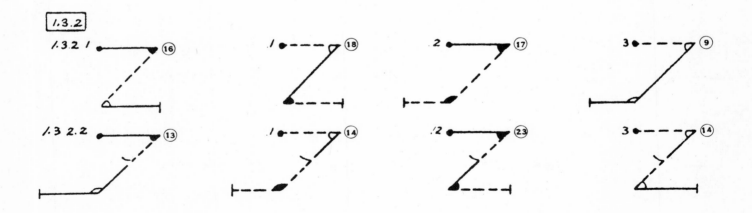

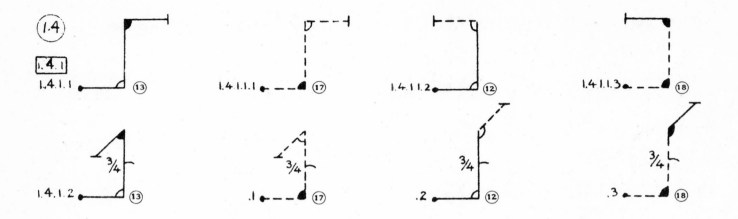

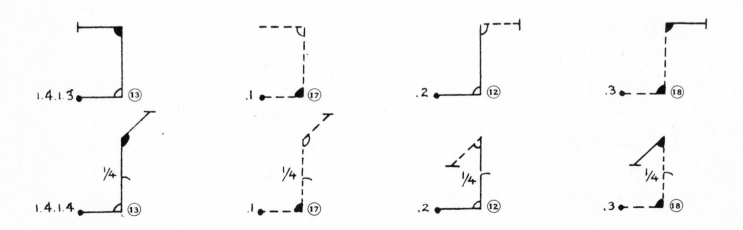

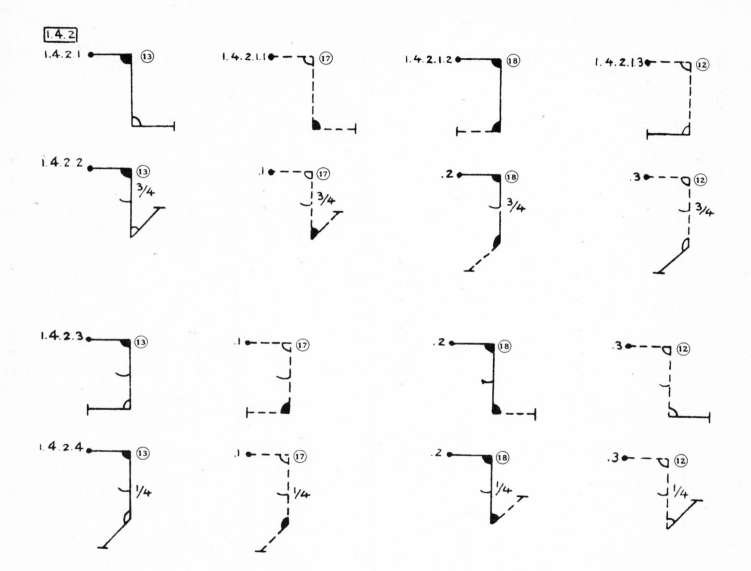

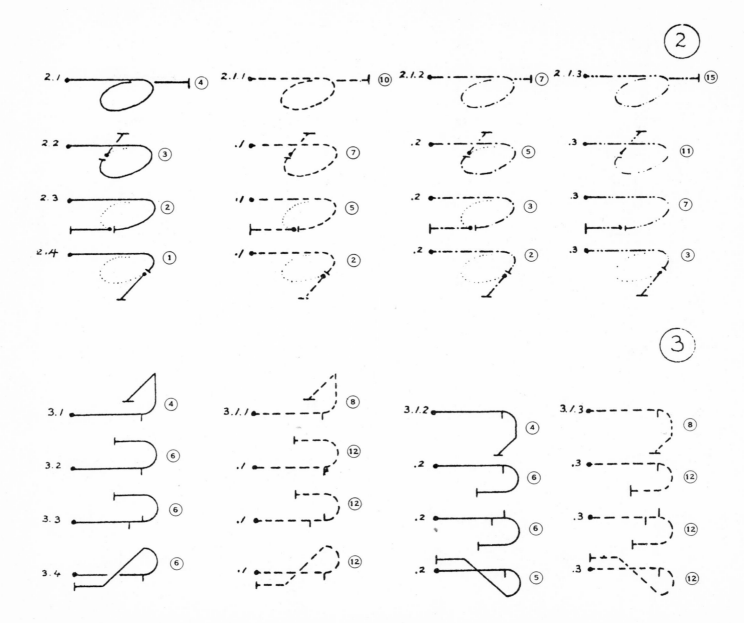

83

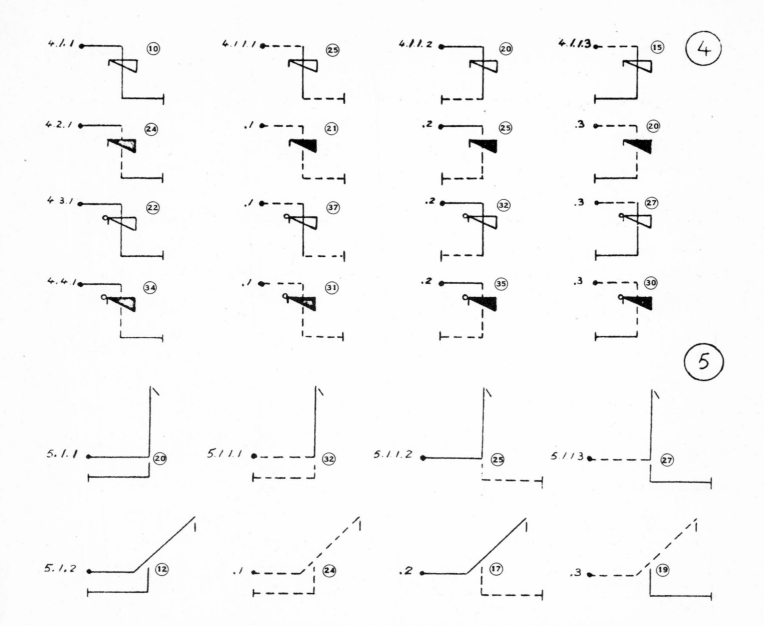

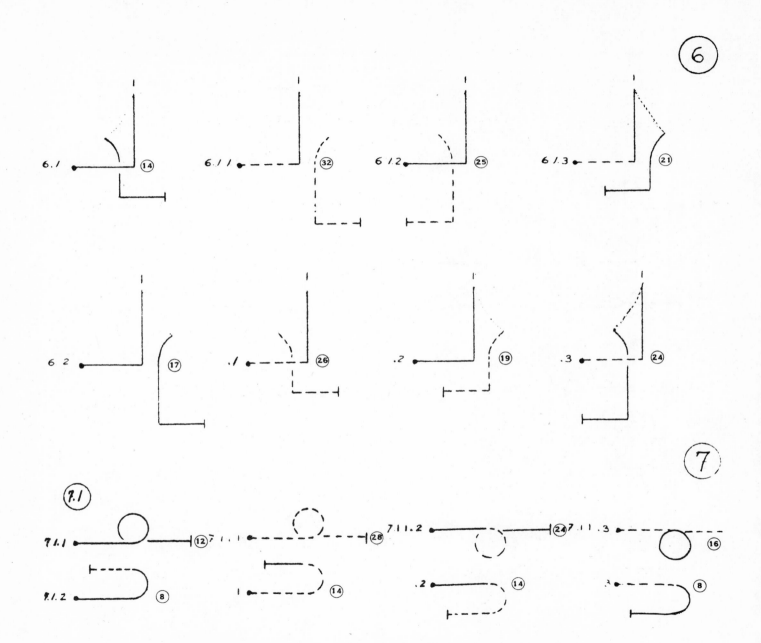

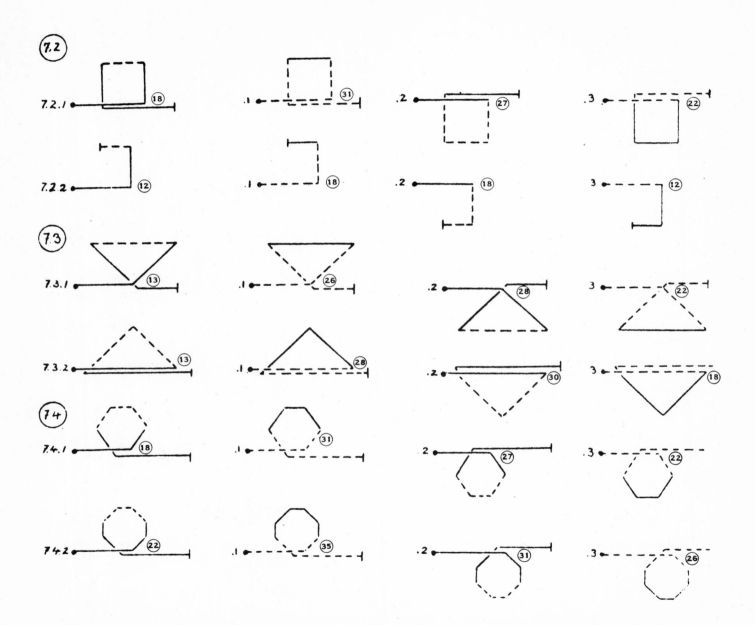

7.2

7.2.1 ⑱

.1 ㉛

.2 ㉗

.3 ㉒

7.2.2 ⑫

.1 ⑱

.2 ⑱

3 ⑫

7.3

7.3.1 ⑬

.1 ㉖

.2 ㉘

3 ㉒

7.3.2 ⑬

.1 ㉘

.2 ㉚

3 ⑱

7.4

7.4.1 ⑱

.1 ㉛

2 ㉗

.3 ㉒

7.4.2 ㉒

.1 ㉟

.2 ㉛

.3 ㉖

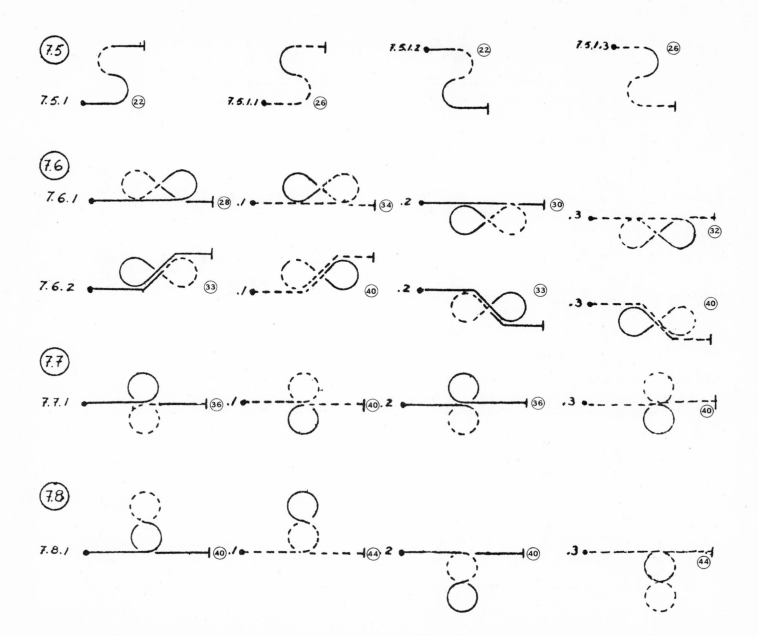

87

88

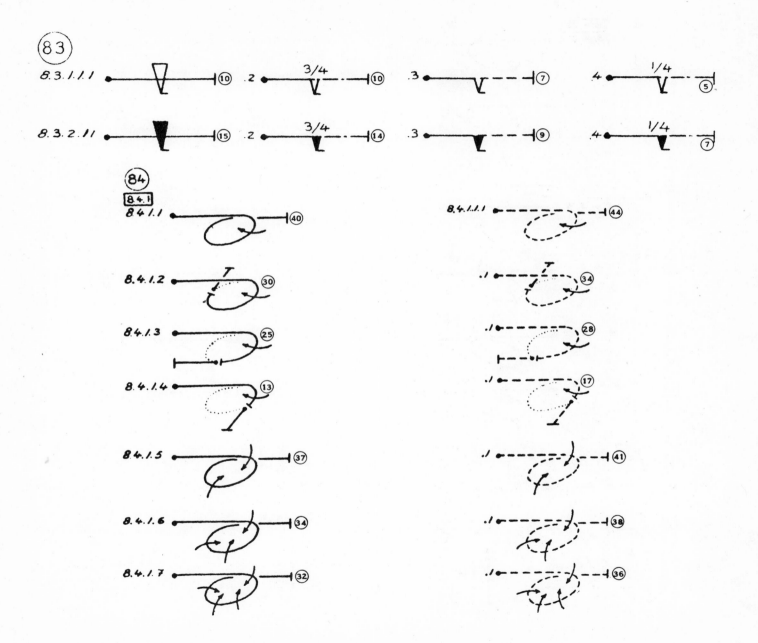

89

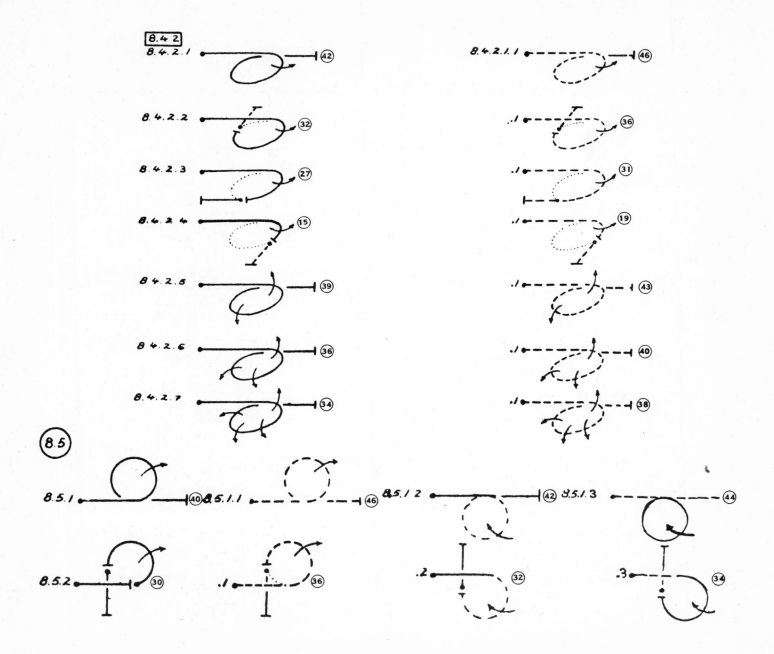

8.4 2

8.4.2.1   (42)   8.4.2.1.1   (46)

8.4.2.2   (32)   .1   (36)

8.4.2.3   (27)   .1   (31)

8.4.2 4   (15)   .1   (19)

8.4.2.5   (39)   .1   (43)

8 4.2.6   (36)   .1   (40)

8.4.2.7   (34)   .1   (38)

8.5

8.5.1   (40)   8.5.1.1   (46)   8.5.1 2   (42)   8.5.1 3   (44)

8.5.2   (30)   .1   (36)   .2   (32)   .3   (34)

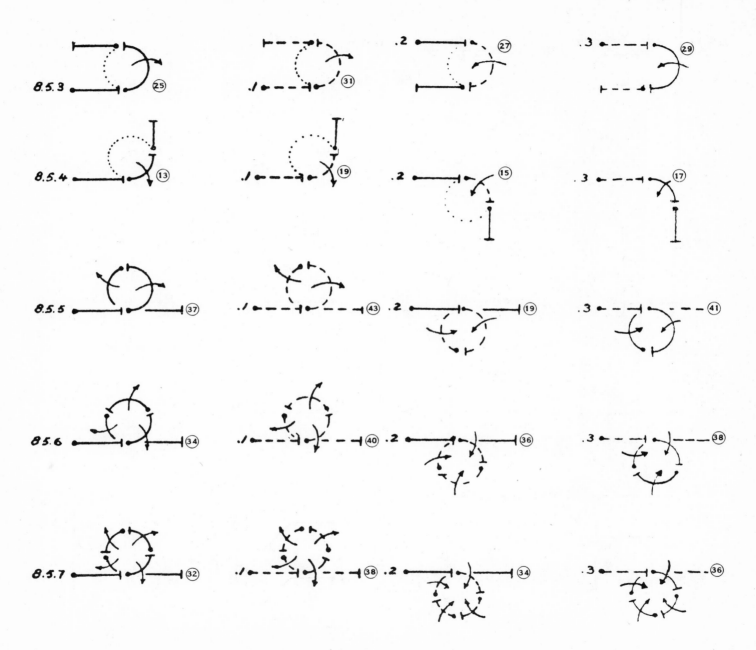

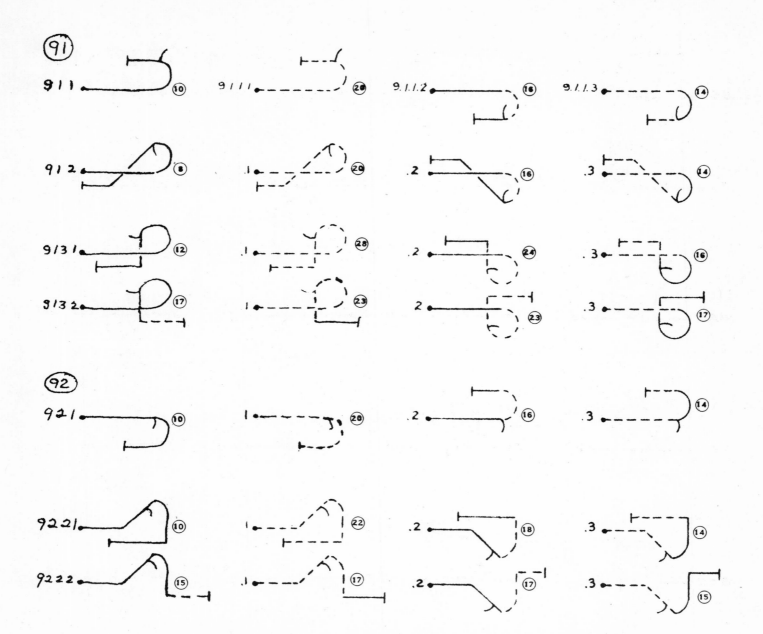

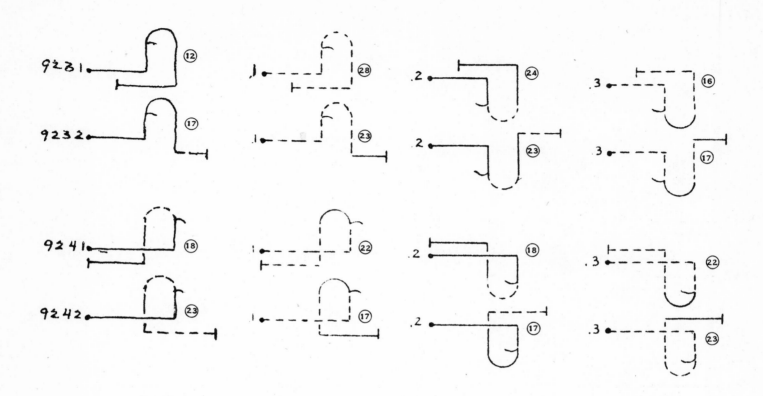